It's No Accident

It's No Accident

*Breakthrough Solutions to Your Child's Wetting,
Constipation, UTIs, and Other Potty Problems*

STEVE J. HODGES, MD,

WITH SUZANNE SCHLOSBERG

LYONS PRESS
Guilford, Connecticut
An imprint of Rowman & Littlefield

Lyons Press is an imprint of Rowman & Littlefield.

Illustrations on pages 5, 62, 67, 72, 75, and 115 by Annemarie B. Johnson, CMI Medical Illustrator.
Illustrations on pages 186, 189, 192, 193, 194, and 195 by Béatrice Favereau.
Thank you to Project CLEAN for the artwork on page 151.

Distributed by NATIONAL BOOK NETWORK

Library of Congress Cataloging-in-Publication Data is available on file.

ISBN 978-0-7627-7360-2

Printed in the United States of America

To my children and patients, who have taught me more about toileting than any textbook or classroom ever did.

To my wife for her love and support.

To my parents for devoting their lives to making mine better.

And to Dr. Sean O'Regan, the smartest guy I know.

CONTENTS

Introduction

Shortly after Thanksgiving in 2010, Zoe Rosso and her mom, Betsy, were escorted off the premises of Zoe's school in Arlington, Virginia. They were told by the principal not to come back for a month, or until Zoe stopped having potty accidents. Zoe had wet her pants more often than the school allowed—the limit was eight times in a month—and therefore was considered "not potty trained." Zoe was three and a half years old.

The incident made the front page of the *Washington Post*, attracted national media attention, and incited some of the most hostile and foolish comments that, as a physician and parent, I have ever read. Betsy was called a "lazy person who wants to dump the kid off so she can shop and drink Starbucks" and told to "quit blaming others for her failures." One *Washington Post* commenter ranted, "It's narcissistic for parents to insist that their untrained child has to be indulged. A parent's job is to raise a well-socialized, functional member of society."

I have since had the pleasure of meeting Betsy and her husband, Randy, and of treating Zoe, who is now four and a half. I can tell you that Zoe is quite a well-socialized, functional member of society. She's a delightful, inquisitive kid and a model patient. I also can tell you it's not Betsy Rosso who failed; the system failed *her*. I don't mean just the Arlington Public School system, which operates the preschool Zoe attended. Yes, policies like those enforced by her school are misguided, and I've treated countless children who have been harmed by them. But the Rossos also were let down by the medical system, which failed to detect that something actually was amiss with Zoe. It turns out her "accidents" were not accidents at all.

Though the Rossos have been accused of laziness and neglect, in fact they did everything you'd expect from devoted, responsible parents. They worked diligently to potty train Zoe, using techniques Betsy Rosso learned in a workshop run by a developmental psychologist. Zoe achieved dryness in a month, shortly after turning three. When she began having accidents at preschool, a few months later, her parents took her to the pediatrician, who concluded that Zoe's wetting episodes were not unusual and likely related to the stress of starting school.

Later, after Zoe left the school, the Rossos took her to a pediatric urology clinic, where Zoe's urine was tested for infection and her belly was examined. According to the urology report, Zoe's abdomen was soft, with "no masses palpable." The report indicated that Zoe "may have some underlying constipation contributing to her urinary symptoms" but stated that "aggressive evaluation and treatment is not recommended." The report did offer the Rossos the option of having Zoe's abdomen X-rayed, though in conversation the certified nurse practitioner who examined Zoe never mentioned an X-ray, reassuring the Rossos that accidents in potty-trained kids under age five are developmentally normal. According to Betsy, she was told that Zoe may have a small bladder that has "not yet grown to catch up with the rest of her body" and that the cause of Zoe's wetting problems was "likely genetic."

All of this was wrong.

In fact, Zoe was severely constipated. Her entire colon was stuffed with poop, including a mass in her rectum the size of a Nerf basketball. Constipation wasn't "contributing" to her accidents; it was the main cause of them. I requested a simple X-ray of Zoe's belly and saw the giant poop mass for myself. Shortly after that, Zoe began aggressive therapy for constipation, including laxatives and physical therapy to retrain her pelvic-floor muscles. Over the course of treatment she and her family have experienced accident-free periods bookended by setbacks and frustration. Though her bladder continues to spasm, her accidents have become far less frequent. Zoe's case has proven to be among the most difficult I have encountered and illustrates the serious and persistent medical consequences that can develop when "accidents" are dismissed as normal. Despite the challenges Zoe faces, she is finally receiving appropriate treatment, and the cause of her accidents is no longer a mystery. The problem that had plagued the Rossos for more than a year, that prompted Zoe's suspension from school and got her mom pegged as a lazy, selfish narcissist, turned out to be easily diagnosed.

I didn't need to X-ray Zoe to figure out the cause of her accidents. I already knew. I had a strong suspicion when I read the *Washington Post* story, before I ever contacted the Rossos to interview them about school potty policies for this book. And I was certain six months later, when Zoe's parents e-mailed me details about her accidents. It's not that I'm some kind of genius, as my wife frequently reminds me. It's just that I see cases like Zoe's every day at our clinic at Wake Forest Baptist

Health, one of a handful in the country specializing in childhood toileting troubles. Actually, I see these problems virtually every day, about a thousand times a year.

I see kids who potty trained early and easily, "practically by themselves," according to their moms, only to start having accidents at age three or four. I see five-year-old girls with recurrent urinary tract infections (UTIs), even though Mom and Dad are vigilant about keeping their daughter clean and dry. I see seven-year-old boys who wet the bed and are told, "Just be patient—you'll grow out of it." I see kids who experience pain when they pee and kids who need to pee so often that they get in trouble at school and make family car trips impossible. All these problems have the same root cause: These kids are holders. They chronically hang on to poop or pee or both, and this holding habit has, for reasons I explain in this book, caused their bladders to go bonkers.

These kids have something else in common: They're stressed out, and so are their families. Some folks, like the Rossos, have been told to find a new school or have been the subject of ridicule. How's this for callousness: At Zoe's first preschool, her teacher would broadcast, in front of the other parents and children, Zoe's accident tally for the day. At the school that ultimately suspended Zoe, the principal told Betsy Rosso that her daughter had "had enough chances." Says Betsy: "They acted like she was some kind of criminal."

Many folks I meet are wiped out from getting up at three o'clock night after night to change bedsheets. Some parents, assuming their children are wetting their pants for attention or for the sake of rebellion, have lashed out in frustration at their kids and gotten locked in power struggles with them. I meet dads who have blamed their wives for mismanaging the potty-training process and moms who feel they have let down their kids. I regularly treat children who are feeling lonely and left out because they're embarrassed to go on sleepovers with their friends. Perhaps the biggest heartbreakers are the kids who feel as if they are disappointing their parents. One day when Betsy picked Zoe up from school, Zoe told her, "I had four accidents. Don't get upset at me." The Rossos kept telling Zoe, "We know this isn't your fault." But apparently that wasn't the message she was receiving at school.

None of this—the exhaustion and distress, the inconvenience and discomfort—needs to happen. There are straightforward solutions to virtually all childhood toileting problems, and I've presented them in detail in this book. For reasons I discuss in Chapter 1, parents and many medical professionals, even urologists, are unaware of these solutions. I want to change that.

As the Rossos learned, our culture typically has two reactions to potty problems: Either these problems are a failure on the parents' part (a ridiculous notion), or they are not problems at all but rather a normal part of growing up. Parents are often led to believe: Sure, my kids have issues, but they are just kids. They get caught up in playing and forget to go potty. Their bladder hasn't "caught up" to their brain. They wet the bed, but that's typical for their age.

These notions are untrue. Virtually all accidents and recurrent urinary tract infections and, I believe, the majority of bedwetting cases, are symptoms of a silent epidemic of holding. It's an epidemic that is needlessly causing pain and anxiety and costing families and the health-care system massive amounts of money. Parents wait and wait for their children to outgrow their potty problems, and they don't have to. In fact, this delay often makes the troubles worse.

Our epidemic of toileting troubles has multiple causes, including the fiber-deficient Western diet, potty training too early and without stringent follow-up, and the irrational demands and priorities of our schools. It is an enormous and growing problem. Consider:

- Up to 30 percent of kids between the ages of two and ten are chronically constipated,[1] and constipation is a cause of an estimated 3 to 5 percent of all pediatric doctor visits.[2]

- Twenty-five percent of five-year-olds have problems with daytime accidents or bedwetting, and each year, half a million kids visit the doctor for these issues.[3]

- Eight percent of girls have had a urinary tract infection by the age of seven, accounting for one million annual visits to pediatric clinics and 14 percent of all emergency room physician encounters between young girls and ER docs.[4]

---

1 van den Berg MM, Benninga MA, Di Lorenzo C. Epidemiology of childhood constipation: a systematic review. *Am J Gastroenterol.* Oct. 2006;101(10):2401-9.

2 Borowitz SM, Cox DJ, Kovatchev B, et al. Treatment of childhood constipation by primary care physicians: efficacy and predictors of outcome. *Pediatrics.* Apr 2005;115(4):873-7.

3 http://kidney.niddk.nih.gov/statistics/uda/Urinary_Incontinence_in_Children-Chapter12.pdf.

4 Ibid.

Toileting problems are frequently misdiagnosed, as in Zoe Rosso's case, and either undertreated or mistreated when they are discovered. In an astonishing number of cases, a doctor will encounter a run-of-the-mill potty problem and instead suspect a rare disorder, ordering expensive and fruitless medical workups. Often these kids don't get help until their symptoms have reached crisis proportions and they are referred to a clinic like ours. Sometimes they don't get help at all, or get help too late, making their symptoms worse. Untreated, these kids can grow into adults with severe toileting issues and pain with sexual intercourse, among other problems.

When parents learn the simple cause of their child's problems, many are stunned. In our clinic, X-rays confirm 90 percent of potty-trained children with wetting problems or recurrent urinary tract infections are severely constipated, just as Zoe Rosso was. Yet only 5 percent of parents even had an inkling their child was backed up. And while parents of children who hold pee sometimes are aware of the holding, they typically have no idea that the habit can compromise their child's bladder capacity.

It is my goal to bring relief to your family. But I hope to accomplish more. I want to change the way that our culture views toileting troubles. Nobody should have to deal with the blame and stress heaped on Zoe Rosso and her folks. Betsy Rosso was dragged through the mud for approaching the *Washington Post* with her story. I applaud Betsy for going public and fighting for her child. I am grateful to her and Randy for allowing me to include Zoe's case in this book. I hope that the book will help many families like theirs.

HOW TO USE THIS BOOK

You may be tempted to scan the table of contents for your child's condition and flip directly to that chapter. Resist the temptation! To really understand the themes in this book, start by reading Chapter 1: The Potty Problem Epidemic and Chapter 2: Trust Me, Your Child Is Constipated, because they apply to virtually all toileting troubles and provide important background. After that, sure, pick and choose the chapters that seem relevant to your family. Still, I recommend that everyone read Chapter 7: Scary Bathrooms, Foolish Rules, and Other Ways School Can Make a Healthy Kid Sick; Chapter 8: Nutrition for Super Pooping; and Chapter 9: The Potty-Muscle Workout, because these chapters will help all children prevent recurrences.

. . . .

CHAPTER 1

The Potty Problem Epidemic

For most parents, a child's graduation from diapers to underwear ranks high on the list of happy occasions, possibly on par with that great day when your baby starts sleeping through the night. Hallelujah! You're free—from hauling around the diaper bag (not that those Diaper Dude bags aren't cool), from those diaper-pail burps (you know, when you open the lid to drop in a new diaper and the stench escapes), and from hoisting your kid onto the changing table in the supermarket bathroom. After all your efforts, you figure you've earned a promotion to the next stage of parenting, never to return to the diaper aisle at Costco. At least until your next child arrives.

I'm with you: I have three daughters under age five, and I've done my share of diaper changing. Well, my wife might dispute the "my share" part, but let's just say I know all the places poop can hide in little girls' bottoms. I know how awesome it is to leave diapers behind and watch your child gain the confidence and independence that comes with using the toilet. When my oldest was first trained, she'd shriek, "See, there it is!" demanding that we inspect and pay tribute to the yellow specimen in the toilet. So I can well understand the anxiety, even despair, you may feel when it all starts to go sideways, when your "big kid" starts peeing in her pants—or worse, pooping in them. Or when your little guy skips a birthday sleepover because he's been wetting the bed.

In addition to worrying about your child—Is he regressing? Could he have a serious illness?—you may feel isolated, as if yours is the only family coping with these messy and sometimes embarrassing problems. Parents tend to broadcast their children's sleep struggles—they'll blog about their baby's 2:00 a.m. cry-a-thons or their sleep-training bible or favorite white-noise machine. But at the playground you don't hear, "Payton pooped in her pants yesterday and the weird thing was, she didn't even notice." No one posts on Facebook: "My second grader wet the bed *again*."

In our culture, it's the toileting troubles that carry a stigma. Few blame Mom when her six-month-old wakes up twice a night—friends and strangers empathize and offer advice. But as Betsy Rosso discovered, parents whose kids have potty problems often are held responsible. Even when fellow parents offer support, as many did to the Rossos when news of their daughter's preschool suspension went viral, guidance is in short supply. Anyone who wants help with sleep issues or potty training can choose from among hundreds of books, DVDs, and seminars. Yet there's virtually no help for solving problems that occur *after* the diaper days. Every day I hear from parents who have scoured the Internet for solutions and come up empty.

My goal is to fill in the knowledge gap. There's a big void, and this is a big problem. Potty accidents may not be topic number one at your annual block party, but trust me: Probably one third of the potty-trained kids on your street are constipated, and chances are, a huge number of them are having accidents, bedwetting episodes, frequency problems, or urinary tract infections because of it. Some parents wait and wait for their kids to outgrow these episodes, assuming that they're a normal, if bothersome, part of childhood. Other parents, concerned that something serious is wrong, take their kids to the doctor, either to be told, like the Rossos, that all is fine or to be prescribed therapies that don't work. I'm telling you: In virtually all cases, toileting troubles have simple causes—namely, holding poop or pee or both—and most can be cleared up within a few weeks or months, though a small percentage of cases, like Zoe Rosso's, are more stubborn.

So you may be wondering: If my kid's problems are a dime a dozen and the solutions are so straightforward, why haven't I heard about these remedies before? Surely you also wonder how your child developed these problems in the first place and why they are so widespread. In this chapter I explain why the proven link between constipation and urinary problems gets so little attention from physicians. It's an instructive story about how medical discoveries can be lost and found again and involves a clever Irish doctor with a constipated son.

In this chapter I also explain the multiple reasons that toileting troubles are epidemic in Western culture and, alarmingly, on the rise. Among these reasons: too many fries and not enough exercise, the rush to get our kids potty trained, and the absence of parental follow-up in the post-diaper days. Parents cringe when I say this, but getting your child out of diapers is the easy part! Culprits also include the many school-related catastrophes, from preschools requiring three-year-olds to be potty trained to grade schools discouraging bathroom breaks to middle schools and high schools with such deplorable restroom conditions that kids hold their pee and poop all day. Some kids, because of their temperaments or genetic makeups, are less affected than their peers by these factors and manage to avoid potty problems. However, enough forces in our culture conspire against healthy toileting behaviors that few children emerge from potty training totally unscathed, and many, many kids, more than you can possibly imagine, end up with whacked-out bladders.

The Patient Who Changed Everything

At some point in his career, every doctor ends up with a case that makes him rethink all he has been taught, a patient who inspires him to look at his field in an entirely different way. For me, that patient was a precocious six-year-old named Ella. She had been referred to our clinic by her pediatrician because of a history of UTIs accompanied by fever, a classic symptom of urinary reflux. Indeed, that was my diagnosis for Ella. Normally, urine flows downward from the kidneys in the two ureters to the bladder, emptying out the urethra and into the toilet. (See Figure 1-1 on page 5.) It's a one-way street. But in kids with urinary reflux, the flap valve at the junction of the

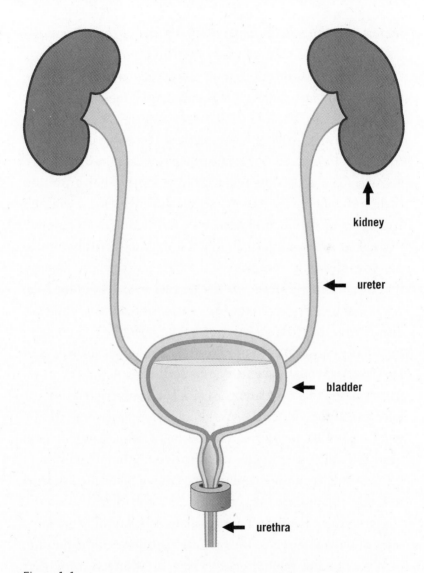

Figure 1-1

In the normal urinary tract, the urine is produced by the kidneys, flows down the ureters to the bladder, and empties through the urethra.

ureters and the bladder is faulty and some of the urine flows back up into the kidneys when the child pees. This creates a yo-yo effect, and the child never completely empties. For reasons I explain in Chapter 5, this poor emptying leads to UTIs and fever.

Now, urinary reflex has long been considered a genetic condition. In most kids it eventually resolves on its own. If you just give the bladder and ureters a few years, they will grow into their appropriate orientation and the valve will begin working appropriately. While urologists wait for these kids to outgrow the reflux, we typically prescribe a low dose of antibiotics to prevent infections and protect the kidneys from the damage that infections with fever can cause. That's what I did for Ella.

But she didn't get better. For various reasons, reflux is far likelier to resolve if a child is not holding her pee and poop, so I redoubled my efforts with Ella. I made sure that she was peeing like clockwork every few hours and that she wasn't constipated, instructing her parents to give her a laxative if she didn't have a soft poop every day. You know what happened? Nothing. In fact, Ella got worse. She developed urinary urgency, the need to rush to the bathroom. This was monumentally frustrating for Ella and her parents, since they'd all worked so hard to follow the program I'd prescribed. I was baffled.

According to what I'd been taught, Ella's only remaining option was surgery. The operation, called reimplantation, involves moving the ureters to a new location, ensuring that the valve works. It's not a particularly risky or difficult surgery, and I'd performed hundreds of them. But because Ella's folks were following my therapies so diligently and because her case didn't seem so severe, I didn't feel I should have to operate. Despite our reputations, surgeons actually aren't eager to cut open every patient who walks through the door. I believed I should have been able to solve Ella's case with laxatives and behavioral management—or at least keep it from getting worse.

I went ahead with the surgery and was startled when I cut open Ella's abdomen. Her intestines were chock full of poop! A grapefruit-size mass of stool was sitting right behind her bladder and squishing it into a position more likely to cause reflux. Despite all my efforts and her parents' attentiveness, Ella had become supremely constipated. To prevent this very scenario, I'd even had her parents fill out multiple questionnaires designed to detect constipation, and Ella had passed them all with flying colors. And still, we'd all missed it. I completed the surgery, and Ella's reflux resolved. But given how much poop she had pressing on her bladder, I felt certain that an intestinal clean-out would have done the job just as well and for a far smaller cost—physically, emotionally, and financially—to Ella and her family. At the very least, she'd have had had a better chance of outgrowing urinary reflux on her own.

Ella's case made me rethink how we detect constipation, which not only contributes to urinary reflux but also is a known cause of UTIs, pee and poop accidents, and bedwetting. I thought: It doesn't help to ask parents or kids how often they're pooping or what their poop looks like. Pressing on a child's abdomen in search of a poop mass, as I routinely did with my patients, also adds little to the picture. I realized we needed something more definitive.

After Ella's surgery I undertook some minor detective work. Using a standard questionnaire, I made a practice of asking parents whether their children showed signs of constipation. Then, for comparison, I'd send these kids for an abdominal X-ray, which would show very clearly whether their intestines were clogged. I did this with all my patients who had recurrent UTIs and daytime or nighttime wetting problems. Among the first fifty patients I X-rayed, all had normal pooping habits, according to the questionnaire results. Yet the films showed that every last one of these kids was stuffed full of poop. I was blown away.

I thought I'd made an epic discovery, like the doctors who figured out that stomach ulcers are caused by bacterial infections, not stress. I thought I could finally prove to my wife I was a genius. As it turns out, my "discovery" had already been discovered—thirty years earlier.

The Mysterious Case of the Bedwetting Five-Year-Old

In the early 1980s, the five-year-old son of Dr. Sean O'Regan, an Irish pediatric kidney specialist practicing in Montreal, was wetting the bed every night, sometimes two or three times. Often the boy would wake his parents; Dr. O'Regan, accustomed, as doctors are, to operating on minimal sleep, would get the elbow from his wife to help their son change his pajamas. On occasion, Dr. O'Regan would find the boy on the floor, having vacated his bed in search of some place dry to sleep.

Self-conscious about the wetting, the boy didn't want to sleep anywhere but home, and this caused a fair amount of tension in the family. Dr. O'Regan was bewildered by the wetting, as his other two sons had achieved overnight dryness by age two or three. As spouses of physicians are prone to do, Mrs. O'Regan made note of the fact that the good doctor was unable to help his own son.

At this time, childhood urinary problems such as bedwetting, daytime accidents, and UTIs generally were considered to be bladder disorders caused by anatomical problems, such as an excessively narrow bladder neck. Children who wet the bed also were thought to have psychological problems. Dr. O'Regan didn't accept either explanation and began searching for answers at the McGill University Medical Library, whose renowned collection included European medical journals dating to the early nineteenth century. He was surprised by what he found: several references, published as far back as the 1890s, to a connection between constipation and urinary problems. A study published in 1968 had demonstrated that children with severe constipation experienced a high rate of urinary problems, suggesting that, contrary to the conventional wisdom, peeing and pooping were intimately related. Also in the 1960s, researchers had found that kids with Hirschsprung's disease, a congenital blockage of the large intestine that causes severe constipation, typically developed all sorts of urinary problems.

Dr. O'Regan felt he was onto something. So he had a colleague, Dr. Salam Yazbeck, test his son's colon using a balloon-inflation procedure called anal manometry. The procedure would determine if, and how extensively, the boy's colon had been stretched by a buildup of stool, the most reliable indicator of constipation. Using a catheter, Dr. Yazbeck inserted a small balloon into the child's bottom and gradually inflated it, waiting for the boy to report discomfort. But the boy felt nothing. Dr. Yazbeck reported to Dr. O'Regan, "The kid's got no rectal tone."

And so the nighttime routine at the O'Regan household included something new: enemas. In fact, Dr. O'Regan gave his son so many Fleet enemas—every night for a month, every other night for a second month—that he negotiated a discount with his local pharmacy. The boy would read *Winnie the Pooh* on his bed while waiting for the action to start. Within a week, he was having his first dry nights. Within two months, he'd stopped wetting the bed completely. Mrs. O'Regan was pleased with her husband.

Based on this success, Drs. O'Regan and Yazbeck began a series of studies at the University of Montreal, Hôpital Sainte-Justine, where they practiced. They got the word out to local pediatricians and attracted virtually the entire French Canadian population of children with urinary problems. Advancing the 1960s research in a significant way, their studies showed that constipation was a major cause of urinary problems in children and that treating the constipation resolved these problems in dramatic fashion.

In one investigation, published in 1985,[5] Dr. O'Regan tracked forty-seven girls, average age eight, who had recurrent

5 O'Regan S, Yazbeck S, Schick E. Constipation, bladder instability, urinary tract infection syndrome. *Clin Nephrol.* Mar 1985;23(3):152-4.

UTIs and also were shown by several scientific measures to be severely constipated. In addition, most of these girls had chronic poop accidents (encopresis) and/or wetting (enuresis). Dr. O'Regan prescribed the same therapy that he'd used on his own son: daily enemas for a month, followed by a month of enemas every other day, followed by a third month of twice-weekly enemas. Within three months, forty-four of the forty-seven girls no longer were having UTIs. Among the twenty-one patients with encopresis, twenty stopped having poop accidents. What's more, twenty-two of the thirty-two girls with enuresis stopped wetting. What about the girls who didn't improve? Almost all their parents admitted to not following the enema regimen fully.

Interestingly, Dr. O'Regan noted in his UTI paper, when he asked the parents of these girls whether their daughters were constipated, nearly half said absolutely not. These folks were in the dark even though the air-filled balloon testing showed the girls' rectums, like his son's, had become severely stretched from holding excess poop. A child with normal rectal sensation would notice a balloon filled with just 5 to 10 milliliters of air, but the girls in Dr. O'Regan's studies did not even sense the balloons until they had been pumped up with 40 milliliters. Every girl in the study could withstand 80 to 110 milliliters of air without discomfort. At 110 milliliters, the balloons were fully inflated, to about 7 centimeters in diameter, roughly the size of a small canteloupe.

This finding tells you why constipation is so easily missed. Often, the rectum simply expands to compensate, like a squirrel's cheeks or a snake's belly. You get the picture. So much poop builds up in the rectum that even though the child may still be able to poop regularly, she never completely empties. Many kids who are severely clogged up poop daily, fooling their parents and doctors into thinking all is fine, intestinally speaking.

Dr. O'Regan was just getting started. Feeling certain that constipation was at the root of childhood urinary problems and that the conventional treatments were useless, he continued to publish studies. One of these involved seventeen children, average age six,[6] who had been diagnosed with urinary reflux, the same condition for which I had performed surgery on Ella. Of these kids, ten also had frequent pee accidents and five had frequent poop accidents. (Ella, as it happened, had neither.) All seventeen children in the study proved to be severely constipated, and most could tolerate the rectal balloon inflated to the max. Dr. O'Regan noted that this poop burden was altering the bladder anatomy in such a way that it was preventing resolution of the reflux. He believed that by treating the constipation, many of these kids could be cured without drugs and surgery. And yet today, more than twenty-five years later, what are the two treatments that urologists typically offer kids with urinary reflux? Drugs and surgery.

Despite all the work by Dr. O'Regan and his colleagues, the therapies for common toileting problems—daytime wetting, bedwetting, poop accidents, UTIs, and too-frequent

6   O'Regan S, Schick E, Hamburger B, Yazbeck S. Constipation associated with vesicoureteral reflux. *Urology*. Nov 1986;28(5):394-6.

urges to pee—also have been, more or less, stuck in time. In the years following publication of O'Regan's studies, urologists and pediatricians began to recognize that constipation is a significant contributor to urinary problems, but they generally did not take sufficient measures to diagnose constipation. They simply asked parents whether their children were pooping regularly. Since most constipated children do poop daily or every other day, this recognition solved few problems.

It seems that many in my profession did not read the O'Regan studies carefully enough, missing the parts where Dr. O'Regan indicated that constipation is routinely missed and is associated with a stretched-out rectum, not the frequency of poops. If you go back and read urology textbooks published over the last thirty years—a really fun way to spend a weekend, if you're looking for ideas—you can clearly see a progression in the recommendations for diagnosing constipation in children, from the 1980 partiality for rectal exam and anal manometry to less and less invasive or aggressive means. Recent publications comment that a thorough physical exam and history from the patient are all that is needed. Some textbooks even recommend against the use of X-rays because they don't correlate well with the frequency and consistency of stool—which is exactly my point!

Because this misunderstanding has been passed down, few doctors seem to diagnose constipation in children who come in with urinary problems or treat constipation aggressively enough when they do find it. They may recommend a small daily dose of laxative, fiber supplements, and frequent trips to the potty and call it a day.

Until fairly recently I was among these doctors. I knew that constipation was a major cause of wetting and UTIs, and so I offered kids the constipation therapies I'd been taught. Unfortunately for my patients these therapies weren't particularly successful. The children I treated continued to have accidents at school or wet the bed or develop UTIs, and this troubled me deeply. I'd prescribe a therapy, and three months later the child and her folks would come back to my clinic, frustrated and exhausted, and I'd have nothing more to offer them.

I couldn't figure out where I was going wrong. Because I'm a urinary specialist, not a gastroenterology (GI) expert, I often would refer these children to gastroenterologists. But these docs would send them right back. I remember a meeting I had with a gastroenterologist about some of my difficult cases. "I don't get it," she said. "These kids you send me—they aren't constipated." She told me that they pooped every day and had normal marker studies. In other words, when they swallowed capsules containing special markers that show up on an X-ray, the poop moved through the colon in a timely manner. (This is a fancier version of the "corn test," which Zoe Rosso's urology clinic suggested that Zoe undergo. You eat corn, much of which is nondigestible, and track how long it takes for little yellow pieces to show up in your poop.)

I scrutinized the X-rays of one of the patients this GI doc had described as "not constipated" and saw a rectum full of poop. That's when it hit me: We have a definition problem.

The conventional understanding of constipation—infrequent pooping—didn't fit. Though some stool was passing through on a daily basis, these kids also were accumulating stool in the rectum. These big, hardened clumps were affecting the bladder in serious ways.

When I started to write up my research findings, I went back and pulled O'Regan's papers. This time I read beyond the summaries, which were readily available online, and dug up the complete articles from the original journals, buried in medical libraries that nobody sets foot in anymore. As it turned out, the finding I thought was so novel—that poop masses in the rectum, not constipation in the "regularity" sense, are a major, unrecognized cause of toileting problems—already had been completely addressed by Dr. O'Regan and then promptly misunderstood by the following generation.

It is a simple semantic error, but one that has caused much suffering. When you actually read Dr. O'Regan's papers, you see that what he meant by *constipation* was a rectum full of poop. He used the term to describe this condition, but apparently many doctors interpreted it in the traditional way. After Dr. O'Regan's papers were published, physicians simply started asking children if they have regular, soft poop, and since most do, even those with a large poop mass in their rectum, the constipation (er . . . rectal burden) was missed. This disconnect became clear to me when I started getting X-rays of my patients.

I was so intrigued by this mammoth miscommunication that I tracked down Dr. O'Regan, who had left Montreal a few years after his papers were published and today treats adults outside of Mesa, Arizona. He was kind enough to answer my questions, and he confirmed my suspicions. When I asked why he thought his message had been ignored, he said he felt that our profession was simply not interested enough in wetting problems to pay attention. "If a discovery is made, and the world wants to take notice, they will. But constipation is a distasteful subject. People don't even want to think about it."

As I began to grasp the true causes of toileting problems and develop my own diagnostic techniques, therapies, and theories based on research in our clinic, I was eager to brainstorm about all this with other pediatric urologists. But like Dr. O'Regan, I encountered a lack of interest. The reality is, urology is a surgical field, and surgeons tend to be fascinated with major reconstructive surgery, like fabricating new bladders out of intestinal tissue for kids with spina bifida. Preschool potty accidents simply don't rate. These problems often resolve with age, so many doctors don't feel an urgency to focus on them, despite the misery experienced in the interim. They tell parents the child has a small bladder and the wetting problems will resolve in a few years. Plus, there are the financial realities: Four-year-olds who wet their pants don't contribute a whole lot to the bottom line, at least not compared to children who require complex operations. Because urologists tend to have little interest in wetting issues, many kids who visit urology clinics are given appointments with physician assistants or nurse practitioners, who may be even less familiar than urologists are with the research linking urinary problems to large rectal poop masses. This happens all the time. In fact, it happened with Zoe Rosso, who was examined at a major pediatric urology clinic by a nurse practitioner. It's entirely possible that Zoe's severe constipation would have been missed by a urologist at the clinic — not an uncommon scenario — but I was not surprised to learn that Zoe had not actually seen a specialist.

Urology clinics aren't the only ones missing the boat. Our patients are referred to us by pediatricians. These frontline docs have to keep up on everything from growth milestones to vision tests to vaccine schedules, so they are often spread thin and may not have the time to delve deeply into the therapies for urinary problems that even urologists know little about. For multiple reasons kids with potty problems are getting shortchanged.

In recent years I have done a complete about-face on my approach to these problems—how I diagnose them, how I treat them, what I believe causes them. I have made toileting problems the heart of my clinical practice and my research.

Back in 1986 Dr. O'Regan had remarkable results with his patients. In one study he followed twenty-two boys and girls with wetting problems.[7] Some of these children had daytime accidents, some wet the bed, and some were plagued by both issues. All were constipated. The parents of seventeen of these children agreed to Dr. O'Regan's favored enema-based

---

7 O'Regan S, Yazbeck S, Hamberger B, Schick E. Constipation a commonly unrecognized cause of enuresis. *Am J Dis Child.* Mar 1986;140(3):260-1.

therapy. By now it won't shock you to learn that all seventeen of these patients improved dramatically. But it may well surprise you to know how quickly their problems resolved: in sixteen days. That was the average. Some of these kids went from wet to dry within three days; for some, recovery took six weeks. Nine months later Dr. O'Regan checked in with his patients. Of the seventeen whose parents had followed through with the enemas, fourteen were still entirely accident free. The other three had gone from having daily accidents to wetting once a week.

At the time of his discovery, Dr. O'Regan told me, he felt pleased that he was able to help so many children who had been blamed for their problems by their parents and had received no more than a shrug from their doctors. "These kids were told that it was all in their heads, that they were psychologically disturbed," he recalled. "When you find something new that actually works, that makes a difference, it's quite spectacular."

Dr. O'Regan noted that he and his colleagues had devoted an immense amount of time to their research and that the one hundred or so children who were tracked for his studies were just a small fraction of the patients he successfully treated with the same methods for the same conditions. Nonetheless, within a decade of the publication of his studies, he told me, his research had been buried. When I asked if he was surprised that someone had dug them up, he said he was not. "It's the rediscovery law of medicine: Things are often lost and recovered again."

Though I can't claim to have made any monumental discoveries, I do, like Dr. O'Regan did back in the 1980s, treat constipation tenaciously, and my clinic gets results. I feel confident that using the therapies described in this book, your family can get results, too.

Why Potty Problems Are Epidemic

The research that Dr. O'Regan and his colleagues pursued a generation ago proved invaluable. These doctors demonstrated that the link between constipation and toileting problems is no coincidence, and that finding was nothing short of revolutionary. But what's behind this connection? How does a mass of poop in the rectum cause a child's bladder to hiccup or cause infections to take root? I discuss various explanations, based on Dr. O'Regan's research and my own studies and experience, in Chapters 2, 3, and 4.

But there are more questions to be answered. We know what causes toileting troubles: holding poop and pee. But what causes the holding? That's an entirely different question from the one that Dr. O'Regan tackled in his day. It is one that I have spent a lot of time thinking about and researching in hopes of figuring out how to prevent these problems and help slow this epidemic. In the next section I address the larger questions: Why are so many kids harboring poop masses and suppressing the urge to pee? And why are these problems becoming even more common?

After studying this problem nonstop for five years, I believe I've pinpointed the three main causes, all intertwined, of this growing epidemic:

- The Western lifestyle, mainly our low-fiber diet and lack of physical activity

- Potty training implemented too early and/or with inadequate follow-up

- The public school system's restrictive toileting policies and, in many cases, crummy facilities

Kids Eat Fries Instead of Fruit

Let's start with diet. You have just brought your new baby home. Congratulations! If you observe closely, you'll see that most of the daily activities that we take for granted are a bit difficult for your newborn. Heck, babies haven't even mastered swallowing; they spit out half of everything you give them! And when they need to pee or poop, you may notice some straining and screaming. This can really frighten parents. I remember watching my oldest daughter, just a few days old, turn beet red just before she'd poop. I would stare intently at her bottom expecting a poop the size of a watermelon to pop out, and instead I'd see a shot of something closer in appearance to applesauce. In most cases these activities are difficult for babies only because they are new to this stuff, but they tend to catch on quickly. They spit up less, and soon they can pee and poop so effortlessly that it seems that they hardly even notice they are doing it. And as I explain in Chapter 2, that is a good thing.

As long as children get most of their nutrition from breast milk or formula, their poop tends to stay mushy, the consistency of Nutella. (Get ready for lots of food metaphors; doctors love them.) And kids squeeze out these soft poops like champs. Life is good! But then they start real food, which for most babies and toddlers means cow's milk and whatever Mom and Dad have picked up from the supermarket. This is the earliest time we see pooping problems develop.

As we all know, the modern Western diet is highly processed, seriously lacking in fruits and vegetables, and therefore deficient in fiber. (In Chapter 8 I explain what exactly fiber is and why it's essential for good pooping.) This is especially true of the foods aggressively marketed to kids. Check out the "kids' menu" at popular restaurants: chicken tenders, hamburgers on white buns, mac and cheese, grilled cheese on white bread . . . with fries! And an Oreo cookie shake! Everyone knows that our kids' eating habits are causing childhood obesity rates to skyrocket—rates have tripled since the 1970s—but what folks don't realize is that our kids' junk-food habits also are a major cause of constipation. A child doesn't need to be packing extra poundage to suffer the effects of eating too many fruit-flavored gummy snacks. (Most brands contain no actual fruit or fiber, but never mind!)

Because kids aren't eating enough fiber, their poop gets firm, and once it gets firm, it gets painful. And pain is the catalyst for the vicious cycle of holding poop. Just like you and me, kids hate pain, so even before they are toilet trained, they can start holding their poop if they think that letting it out may hurt. I used to believe babies and toddlers could not get constipated before toilet training. Well, I was wrong, and I have the X-rays to prove it.

Kids Toilet Train Too Early

Even before toilet training, many children are withholding or reluctantly pushing out large, hard stools and getting constipated. This constipation, as I will later describe in more detail than you ever wanted, can have a profound effect on a child's ability to stay dry during the day and night. Most children who have difficulty with toilet training are constipated before their little bottoms ever even hit the potty chair.

If your child is fortunate enough to avoid constipation before toilet training, either because she's genetically lucky or because she has stellar eating habits, don't worry, because toilet training will fix that! Kids hold their pee and poop because they simply don't understand how essential it is to get yourself to the bathroom when nature calls. Kids think you should only go to the bathroom when you really, really, really need to, or when your mom threatens to withhold television if you don't.

So they put it off. They simply make lousy decisions about when they should pee or poop. This should surprise no one who has children. My two-year-old would walk into oncoming traffic if I didn't stop her, so how could she possibly be trusted to relax her sphincter in a timely manner multiple times a day? Yet somehow it has become popular for one- to two-year-old children to be potty trained. And then there's the "elimination communication" movement, which advocates that newborns bypass diapers altogether and start using the potty shortly after birth, or within a few months of entering the world. Let me tell you: This is nuts.

Parents take pride when their children train early, in the same way they beam when their kids walk, talk, or read before their peers. But you shouldn't think of early toilet training with pride. You should think of it the same way you would if your two-year-old made any other major life decision on her own: with dread. The most seriously constipated children I see in my clinic tend to be those who trained the earliest and with the most ease. In other words, they have been deciding for the longest period of time when they should pee or poop. It's a disaster. I don't want to be dogmatic about the appropriate age to start toilet training, and I discuss this further in Chapter 7, but I've never met a kid younger than three who truly has the mental capabilities to make good toileting decisions. Sure, they can be trained to pee or poop when instructed to sit on the potty, but that's not the same as having enough sense to respond to their bodies' urges in a judicious manner.

Schools Have Restrictive Bathroom Policies and Scary Toilets

So once you've got your toilet-trained child who lives on mac and cheese and holds his pee and poop until the very last minute, what's the one thing you could do to make the situation even worse? Yes, put him in a strange, new, structured environment with unreasonable toileting requirements, restrictive bathroom policies, and possibly frightening and/or filthy toilets that may not even have doors. You know: school.

For starters, you have preschools, day cares, and summer camps that won't accept three-year-olds in pull-up diapers, forcing parents to train their children in many cases before the kids are ready. Then the children graduate, and it's on to grade school, where they are offered root beer–flavored milk at lunchtime and virtually no opportunity to engage in the kind of physical activity that keeps their insides humming along. Did you know that only about one-third of elementary children have daily P.E., and less than one-fifth have extracurricular physical activity programs at their schools? But those problems pale in comparison to the rampant fear of school bathrooms.

Now, I'm kind of a goofball for a doctor. I like childish humor and tasteless jokes, so naturally I enjoyed the movie *American Pie*. As you may or may not recall, in that fine film there was a character known as Paul Finch portrayed by Eddie Kaye Thomas. He was a kind of a coffee-drinking nerd (like me!). Finch's nickname was "Sh*t-break," because he refused to poop at school. He would hold all day to avoid using the school toilets for "number two." Well, one of Finch's so-called friends solved this problem in a prank involving a bottle of laxatives and a mochaccino, and the scene is pretty darned funny. But from where I sit during my day job, it's not funny at all.

It turns out we have a nation of "Sh*t-breaks," kids who are either too scared, grossed out, or embarrassed to poop or even pee at school. I was one of those kids. At my school if you tried to poop, students would bang on the stall doors or try to open them or throw wet paper towels at you. I was terrified of setting foot in the restrooms.

But bullies are only a small part of the problem. Many schools, concerned that kids will invent any excuse to leave class, have toileting policies that actually punish children for taking bathroom breaks. Wait until you hear from one of my patients, Cici Carter, who developed chronic UTIs after years of avoiding her school bathrooms because of the "mystery smells—like sewage" emanating from them, not to mention the hair-clogged sinks and missing toilet paper, soap, and paper towels. None of this shocked her mom, Dee Carter, an elementary school teacher who is not allowed to give her students more than four bathroom passes per quarter. (You can read about the Carters in Chapter 7.) These policies, combined with our processed food–eating, video game–playing culture, have created quite a problem.

And it's getting worse. A study tracking data in the United States showed that from 1992 to 2004 constipation diagnoses more than doubled at outpatient clinics and quadrupled at hospitals, with children fifteen and under registering the highest number of visits for chronic constipation, at almost the rate of seniors.[8] Johns Hopkins Children's Center reported a 30 percent rise in the number of serious and chronic constipation cases in a short period in the late 2000s, prompting the center to open a clinic, much like our own, dedicated to providing therapy for children with the condition.

------

8   Rajindrajith S and Manjuri N. Constipation in Children: Novel Insight Into Epidemiology, Pathophysiology and Management. *J Neurogastroenterol Motil.* January 2011; 17(1): 35–47.

At Wake Forest Baptist Health, not only are we booked solid with children whose urinary problems are caused by constipation, but we've also found that, as with our country's childhood obesity epidemic, the worst cases are getting worse. Some children's colons have been so stretched out by giant poop masses for so long—think of a python with a goat in its belly—that these kids feel too bloated and are in too much pain to eat. In addition to having urinary problems, a small, unlucky fraction of these children need surgery to remove the segments of their colons so damaged that they appear unable to shrink back to size. Yes, those are extreme cases, but I mention them to hammer home the possible consequences of ignoring constipation.

So there you have it. The rest of this book explains how to undo the damage and get your child back on track, so that years from now, all these messy problems will have long been forgotten.

Chapter 2

Trust Me, Your Child Is Constipated

I've upset more than a few parents after evaluating their children for wetting issues and then sending the family home with a therapy for constipation. "But my child isn't constipated" is a common response, followed by, "What does constipation have to do with accidents, anyway?" Just the other day a mom whose seven-year-old son chronically wet the bed and had a history of hard, infrequent poops insisted that I prescribe bladder medication for her son. I explained that clearing up constipation is a necessary first step and medication a last resort that may actually exacerbate constipation. She promptly told the checkout nurse that she wasn't going to bring her son back for follow-up.

This happens all the time, and I can understand why parents are skeptical. The connection between pooping problems and wet undies isn't obvious or well-known. So if you picked up this book because you've already guessed your child is carrying around a jumbo load of poop, kudos to you. You're ahead of the game. Actually, as I explain in Chapter 1, you're ahead of many pediatricians and urologists. (Have you considered enrolling in medical school?) Even if your son or daughter is the rare child with wetting problems who isn't constipated, it's actually helpful to assume he or she is. Making your child's poops softer or more regular can only help resolve bladder issues. So keep reading.

In this chapter I explain how having a pelvis full of poop can make a child's bladder misfire, and I cover the telltale signs that a kid is stopped up. Many of these red flags will surprise you. And finally, the section you've been waiting for: a plan for getting your child's colon unclogged.

What Constipation Really Means

The main reason constipation is overlooked as a cause of wetting problems is confusion over the definition of the word. What does constipation mean to you? You probably associate the term with pooping infrequently, perhaps less often than every other day, like when you get stymied on vacation after taking three flights and adjusting to a new time zone. This definition of constipation is spot on when you're talking about adult bowel problems. Older folks are especially prone to constipation; that's why their bathroom counters look like pharmacy shelves featuring every laxative known to humankind. Their bowel muscles, like their biceps, aren't as robust as they used to be and have lost some of the oomph necessary to move things along.

But this scenario hardly applies to three-year-olds. Virtually all kids have perky intestines. What's more, for reasons I'll explain shortly, many constipated kids actually poop frequently. I can't count the number of constipated four-year-olds I've evaluated who poop three or more times a day. These kids are "regular," all right, yet they're hauling around a belly load of poop.

So forget the conventional definition of constipation. Delete! Instead, when it comes to kids, think of constipation as carrying a "poop burden," as doctors like to call it. (Actually "fecal load" is what doctors really like to call it, but I'll spare you that bit of jargon.) An X-ray is the most accurate way to diagnose constipation, as I explain in the section titled, "When to Get Your Child X-Rayed for Constipation (And Why It's Safe)." And I do frequently order X-rays for children whose constipation is not obvious or whose parents want visual evidence. Still, you don't necessarily need a picture of a child's colon to figure out whether it's stuffed with poop.

In my experience the most telling symptom is a tendency toward extra-large bowel movements. You know something is out of whack when your kid's poops are bigger than your own (sorry to involve our own poop in this). This happens when children delay pooping, even just a bit and even just once in a while. Gradually stool piles up in the end of the colon, known as the rectum. When it's finally forced out— when the kid can't hang onto it any longer and sprints to the toilet in the middle of dinner—what you're looking at is a two-flusher, maybe even a call-Roto-Rooter-toilet-clogger. One mom told me her daughter's XXL poops stopped up the toilet so often that she established a rule: no flushing without first summoning Mom or Dad so a grown-up could be ready with a plunger. Once, the parents even had to cut the poop down to size with a butcher knife!

If poop size is the top predictor of constipation, firmness—a well-formed log or small, hard pebbles—is a close second. As one dad put it, "My kid poops big ol' turkey sausages. What comes out of his bottom you could pick up and put on the grill." What most adults don't realize is that human poop isn't supposed to resemble a Polish kielbasa. When adults have firm poops, due to a low-fiber diet or inactivity, we can get away with it because we usually empty our bowels in a timely manner. But since kids tend to hold their poop, for reasons I'll get to shortly, it's essential that their stools stay soft. Poop is supposed to be mushy, like pudding or a thick milkshake or a fresh cow patty. Gross enough for you? Most people would consider a puddinglike poop too soft, possibly even an indication of illness. Moms of my preschool-age patients often hear from teachers, "Ethan had a loose poop today—he might be coming down with something." Of course that loose poop is exactly what I tell moms to aim for.

To see what a perfect poop looks like, check out the Bristol Stool Scale (Figure 2-1 on page 37). Yes, believe it or not, some folks in England actually stopped listening to good music and eating bad food long enough to produce a pictorial representation of the various forms of poop. It has been proven that poops numbers 1 through 3, with fun descriptions such as "sausage-shaped but lumpy," are typical of constipation, whereas 4 through 6—"soft blobs" and "fluffy pieces"—are not. Seven is diarrhea, but you didn't need a picture to figure that out. When I suggest to parents that they hang the scale on their fridge, they look at me in shock and horror. This is followed by relief when I say, "Just joking!" (Like I said, I have a childish sense of humor.)

In all seriousness, though, I do suggest hanging this chart in the bathroom. Instruct your child to scrutinize each poop he produces, find the corresponding number on the chart, and report back to Mom or Dad. Some kids, usually boys, actually think this is totally cool stuff. (These tend to be the same kids who think boogers and farts are hilarious as well. I was one of those kids.) If your child is too young to reliably connect a number with his poop, assign one-word descriptions to each type of stool. One of my four-year-old patients tells his parents when he has done a "rock poop" (not good), a "log poop" (somewhat better), or a "smush poop" (high five).

Though supersize and/or firm poops are surefire signs of constipation in a child, there are many other, more subtle warnings. We list these in the box, "Eleven Signs Your Child Is Constipated" on page 34.

When to Get Your Child X-Rayed for Constipation (And Why It's Safe)

Bailey Hooten, the mom of one of my patients, was stunned when I told her that constipation was causing her son's bedwetting. I'm not even sure she believed me—before I showed her an X-ray of Jack's belly.

"Until you actually look at the film, it's hard to understand," Bailey says. "I was blown away. Jack was so stuffed with poop that his bladder was basically flattened. I could totally see why pee could not stay in there all night."

Even a severely constipated child can have a belly that looks and feels normal. When I examined him, Jack Hooten was a wiry second grader with a flat abdomen. I saw no bloating and felt no hard mass. But I ordered an X-ray for him, because even inside a small body, there's plenty of room for poop to hide.

I know from my research and experience how unhelpful a physical exam is. For example, in a study conducted at my clinic we looked back at thirty children, average age nine, who were chronic bed wetters. Based on their histories and clinical exams, only three of these kids, 10 percent, were considered constipated. But X-rays showed that twenty-four of the kids, 80 percent, were clogged with poop. Put another way, 87.5 percent of the children who were shown via X-ray to be constipated had no outward signs of constipation.

I realize that parents are wary of exposing their children to radiation, particularly for a condition as seemingly harmless as constipation. We're not talking about a broken leg, after all. But broken legs heal in six weeks. I would argue that for kids with wetting problems, getting an accurate diagnosis of constipation—a problem that can cause years-long, even lifelong, suffering—is crucial.

The radiation dose of an abdominal X-ray, known as a KUB (for kidneys, ureters, and bladder) is the same dose you get from simply living for three months. I think that in many cases, an X-ray is perfectly reasonable. I typically order a second X-ray when a constipated child's symptoms have not improved after a month or two of therapy. The picture helps me decide whether more aggressive treatment of the constipation is warranted or whether the child's colon is clear and we should try bladder-relaxing medication (which, as I explain in Chapter 3, can have many downsides).

The use of X-rays for constipation is a charged issue, and I am absolutely opposed to the overuse of X-rays in children. You'd have to threaten me with a baseball bat to get me to order a CT scan in a kid. But the amount of good you can do for a child with bladder problems by accurately diagnosing constipation far outweighs the risks of a couple of plain X-rays.

Perhaps you are thinking: *Why even bother with the X-rays? Why not just assume all kids are constipated and treat them that way? You won't do any harm, and everyone will get better.* Great in theory, but how would you know when the child is truly cleaned out? Many, many, *many* parents have come to my office swearing their children's colons were as empty as the Lincoln Tunnel at three in the morning. They demand to know why—after the mega laxative clean-out I recommended and all the pooping and diarrhea that ensued—their child is still having wetting problems. Quite often a second X-ray tells them why: Because the kid is still full of poop!

If you absolutely do not want your child X-rayed, you can seek out a radiologist experienced in ultrasound. Discuss this with your pediatrician. An ultrasound of the rectum isn't as quick or easy to read as an X-ray, but it can indicate whether the rectum is, or isn't, full of poop. If your child does end up having an X-ray, make sure your doctor reads it himself, rather than relying on a report from a radiologist. Radiologists don't always comment on stool burden, so they may miss it.

ELEVEN SIGNS YOUR CHILD IS CONSTIPATED

Sometimes there's no doubt a child is clogged up, like when pooping causes obvious pain. You know your kid is constipated if you find her balled up in the corner sobbing every time she needs to go number two. But typically the symptoms are less noticeable. If your child shows at least one of the following signs, she almost certainly is backed up.

1. *Extra-large bowel movements.* If your child's poops are larger than you would expect from a child—more than three quarters of an inch wide and more than six inches long— he almost certainly has been holding it. (Long thin ones that look like garden snakes can be okay.) The large size suggests the poop has extended from his rectum up into his intestines. The width is the key warning sign; poops should be thin!

2. *Firm bowel movements, as opposed to amorphous, gooey poops.* To see what's normal and what's not, look at the Bristol Stool Scale on page 37.

3. *Infrequent bowel movements.* If your child is pooping less often than every other day, she's probably holding her poop. But remember: Daily pooping doesn't rule out constipation. The appearance and consistency are more telling.

4. *Poop accidents.* These usually are caused by overflow from a stretched-out rectum. When the rectum is really full, some poop just drops out. This is called encopresis, and it means stool incontinence.

5. *Poop-stained underwear.* This is often explained away as poor wiping, but it's actually a sign of trouble. Sometimes, when children try to poop with an overly full rectum, they can't push it all out. Incomplete emptying results in less than a clean break, so the child's bottom is harder to wipe. The upshot: skid marks, as eleven-year-old boys and goofy pediatric urologists like to call them.

6. *Super-loose stools.* Wait, isn't it hard poops that signal constipation? Yes, but very loose stools can, too. When you have a large, hard stool burden in your rectum, sometimes looser poop oozes by and finds a way out more easily than the hard stuff. The child may appear to have diarrhea when really she is constipated.

7. *Intermittent, mild belly pain with no obvious cause.* Constipation is the most common source of a tummy ache in kids. This symptom is often dismissed. I've had countless patients complain that their bellies hurt, only to be told by Mom or the pediatrician, "Three-year-olds complain about tummy aches all the time." That's because so many of them are constipated!

8. *Pooping more than twice a day.* In kids with wetting problems, this can be as worrisome as not going at all, because it suggests that the rectum is full of poop and is not being emptied completely. When the rectum is stretched too far it loses its tone and a lot of its strength, like when your child's older, bigger sibling borrows her favorite shirt and stretches it out, so the rectum can't muster the force to evacuate all of the poop.

9. *Continued trouble toilet training.* Children who never quite graduate to "fully toilet trained," whether due to pee or poop accidents, typically are constipated. There's no set amount of time it "should" take to potty train a child, but if you find yourself repeatedly thinking (or worse, saying to your child), *You should know better by now,* there's a good chance she's constipated.

10. *Hiding while pooping in diapers or pull-ups.* Kids who crouch behind the sofa to poop, either before they start potty training or during the process, have a high rate of constipation.

11. *Itchy or painful anus, hemorrhoids, or bleeding with bowel movements.* Some of the signs of constipation are more typical of those seen in adults. If your child has these symptoms, starting therapy is urgent so she doesn't develop an association of discomfort with pooping, which only leads to more holding and is hard to undo.

This handy chart, developed in the 1990s at the University of Bristol in the United Kingdom, can help you distinguish between a healthy poop and one that indicates constipation. If your child's poops resemble Types 1 or 2, your kid is constipated. Types 3 and 4, but especially Type 4, are considered ideal poops. Types 5, 6, and 7 tend toward diarrhea.

- **Type 1:** Separate hard lumps, like nuts (hard to pass)

- **Type 2:** Sausage-shaped, but lumpy

- **Type 3:** Like a sausage but with cracks on its surface

- **Type 4:** Like a sausage or snake, smooth and soft

- **Type 5:** Soft blobs with clear cut edges (passed easily)

- **Type 6:** Fluffy pieces with ragged edges, a mushy stool

- **Type 7:** Watery, no solid pieces, entirely liquid

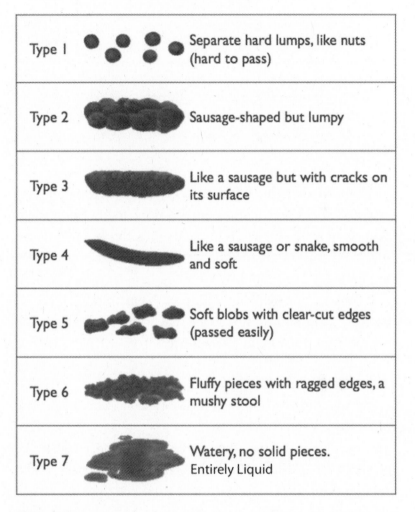

Figure 2-1
The Bristol Stool Scale

The form and size of a poop depend mostly on how much time it spends in the colon. Normally the sandwich a kid eats for lunch exits as poop about twenty-four hours later; in constipated kids, transit time can be over one hundred hours. Typically the delay is in the rectum, the part of the colon that's closest to the bladder, which is why rectal clogs can lead to urinary problems.

Even a doctor who is on the lookout for constipation may miss it if she is not looking in the right place. She should focus on how much poop is in the rectum, the segment of the colon that is right next to the bladder. In children with wetting problems, you typically see a big ball of stool. Children with constipation-related wetting problems rarely empty all the way, so in almost all cases, stool will be evident in the rectum, even if the child just pooped.

How Children Get Constipated

Before your kid was born, you probably took a childbirth class that included a scary video, and maybe you attended a baby-care course that involved diapering a plastic doll. (Really useful, eh?) Well, if I had my druthers, every parent-to-be would enroll in Poop 101, a class covering what exactly should come out of a child's bottom. That way, you'd be prepared to take action at the first sign of constipation, which often happens far earlier than parents realize. Though constipation is epidemic among preschool- and school-age kids, in many children problems start around age one, when babies start drinking milk and eating table food.

At this point their stools become thicker, sometimes resembling pebbles or marbles. A baby's diet—breast milk or formula and baby food—promotes mushy, seedy poop because it's high in water content and breaks down easily. But for reasons that are unclear, cow's milk seems to thicken poop. So does the switch to solid food, especially the foods that toddlers eat, which tend to be low in water content and fiber. Fiber holds onto water as it passes through the bowel, helping stool remain soft; hamburgers and chicken nuggets do not.

In some kids, stools get so thick that they become hard and painful to pass. Think of it this way: For your whole life, squishy poop inconspicuously makes its way out your bottom, and then suddenly a big lump of coal is attempting the same exit strategy. I've known parents so desperate to provide their sobbing babies relief from the pain that—brace yourself!—they've resorted to digging into the child's bottom with the end of a spoon, or a finger, and scooping out the offending mass of rock-hard poop. (I can't recommend inserting hard instruments into a child's bottom, but a gentle finger is okay if necessary. I've done it on plenty of patients.)

Not surprisingly, many children with painful stools begin to willfully withhold their poop even before they are toilet trained. This is simple pain-avoidance behavior, but it makes the problem worse. The next time the child needs to go, the stool is bigger and harder. The upshot: The kid never wants to poop. Among kids who aren't yet potty trained, one sure sign of constipation is hiding—in the corner, behind the couch, in the closet—to poop in their diapers.

Incidentally, for a portion of constipated children, switching from cow's milk to soy milk seems to relieve the constipation, even when laxatives don't. Researchers speculate that these kids may have an allergy to cow's milk protein, and the allergy makes pooping so painful that these kids withhold.

A NEW WAY TO MEASURE CONSTIPATION

Using X-rays to detect a clogged colon and treat wetting problems isn't something doctors have traditionally done, so there are few standardized criteria for diagnosing constipation. For example, just how much poop needs to be stuck in the rectum in order to trigger bladder problems?

The criteria that do exist assess how much stool is in the entire colon, so they are not particularly well suited to helping treat bladder problems. This missing piece prompted a colleague, pediatric radiologist Evelyn Anthony, and I to create a ratio that we think best pinpoints constipation in the rectum and suggests that wetting problems are related to this poop burden. We've named it the Rectal to Pelvic Outlet Ratio (RPOR). (If you have a catchier idea, send it in.) To get a better handle on whether constipation is behind your child's wetting problems, you might suggest that your pediatrician use this calculation when evaluating your child's X-ray.

Have you heard of the "golden ratio" in mathematics and the arts that the ancient Greeks described? Well, here's the golden ratio of poop: the diameter of the rectum at its widest point (the point at which the rectum has been most stretched

Once a child is toilet trained, well, the poop really hits the fan, so to speak. At this stage kids who already are constipated become more so because, pain or no pain, three-year-olds simply do not want to poop. They want to build Lego dump trucks or shop with their toy grocery carts. Even kids who have never been constipated, because they love veggies or have particularly sprightly bowels, hold their poop when they start potty training

out by the mass of poop) divided by the diameter of the outlet of the rectum (the hole in the bones at the bottom of the pelvis).

Now, you might think that all kids have some poop in their rectums, so this ratio doesn't mean squat. Ah, we're one step ahead of you. To eliminate this possibility, we compared twenty-five kids with wetting issues to a random assortment of ninety-three kids who had been X-rayed due to injuries. We found that the injured kids had, on average, a ratio of 0.75—in other words, the poop mass in their colons was far narrower than the exit door. When we looked at kids with urinary problems, the ratio was 1.2! (That's two standard deviations larger than the normal ratio, for those who happened to enjoy their college statistics course.) In plain terms, the ball of poop was wider than the outlet, explaining why these kids don't empty well. Same reason a sofa I once bought got stuck in the doorway into my apartment and I had to return it.

Bottom line: Our study showed that for kids with wetting issues, the most commonly used criteria for identifying constipation in an X-ray were off base. Many of the children in our study had normal scores by conventional standards, because the total amount of poop in their colons was not exceedingly high, but they nonetheless had supersize loads of poop in their rectums.

and often end up constipated. Statistics vary greatly, but anywhere from 5 percent to 30 percent of children ages two to ten are chronically hauling around a load of poop.

The younger a child potty trains, in my experience, the more likely she is to get backed up. I believe that younger, more immature children are less able to understand that it's important to poop right when they get the signal. Also, the earlier a child potty trains, the more months or years she has to develop the holding habit and develop chronic problems. Little research has investigated whether potty training a child early raises her risk of becoming constipated, but our clinic's database supports the idea that it's best to wait. We reviewed the records of almost one hundred children with wetting problems, and the vast majority of them fell into two groups: those who began training before age two (they held their poop and became constipated) and those who trained between three and four after a failed attempt around age two (likely due to constipation during toddlerhood).

The body is designed to poop right when you feel the urge, but kids mostly ignore the initial signal. In addition to having other items on their agenda besides pooping, children tend to be picky about where they poop, avoiding public toilets, including school bathrooms, and/or places they consider dirty or scary. Many kids will poop only at home, which is a prescription for trouble.

If the kid is a trooper and keeps shoving out the poops no matter what the shape or firmness or level of pain involved, no one may notice that anything is wrong, especially if the child keeps pooping almost daily. Most constipated children don't tell their parents or teachers they're having difficulties. In most cases, they don't even realize something is amiss, especially if painful poops are the only kind of poops they've known. Heck, I strained to poop throughout my entire childhood, and it never occurred to me that my experience was abnormal. Considering how few adults know what a healthy bowel movement looks like, it's unlikely any child would have a clue. Plus, once they are toilet trained, kids tend to relish their independence and are not likely to share what's happening in the bathroom. When kids stop needing help wiping, Mom and Dad are even more out of the picture. So even if parents are aware of the signs of constipation, they may not be in a position to know what's coming out of their child's bottom.

Holding behavior can become ingrained in a child's mind and become quite a bad habit. In Chapter 9, we cover strategies to help children unlearn this behavior. No matter what road a child took to constipation, the buildup of poop can lead to all sorts of bladder problems. In the next section I explain why.

How Constipation Causes Bladder Problems

The connection between constipation and bladder problems makes a lot of sense when you consider how holding behavior affects a kid's insides. In the first year of life, when a baby has mushy poop, her colon operates according to design: as a transporting organ. Poop travels along its length, and water, along with nutrients, is slowly absorbed. The stool reaches the end of the colon and moves into the rectum, which is a sensing organ, designed to detect when poop has arrived. (You know what that feels like.) In babies, as the rectum fills it empties by reflex. Those of us who are potty trained need to willfully let it out by relaxing our sphincters, allowing the rectum to evacuate the poop into the toilet. (Apologies for the visuals!) If you do this in a timely manner, you have regular, soft, small bowel movements, and you shouldn't need to wipe much, because each time you go, you empty the rectum completely.

However, the colon wasn't designed to handle turkey sausages. Thousands of years ago—when early humans never delayed pooping longer than it took to squat and they were roaming the plains and eating berries instead of playing Xbox and scarfing down Doritos—all our poops were soft. But that's hardly the case today. The processed, low-fiber foods we eat routinely are detained in the rectum until the ideal time to poop, like when you are at home in your private bathroom with quilted two-ply toilet paper.

Why is this a problem? Imagine an assembly line with the slowest worker at the end. All the products pile up at that point and then start backing up. Remember the candy factory scene from *I Love Lucy* when Lucy and Ethel tried to keep up with the runaway conveyor belt and ended up stuffing candies into their blouses, caps, and mouths? (No? Look it up on YouTube!) That's essentially what is happening inside a constipated child's rectum. She holds in the poop by squeezing her sphincter, converting her colon and rectum into storage units, a job these organs are not suited for. When a child lets her rectum get stretched often enough, she loses her ability to sense that it's ready to empty. It's like if your house is always cluttered: After a while you don't even notice the logjam of laundry baskets and the mail piled up on the table, so you don't clean up, even when your mother-in-law comes over.

Making matters worse, after the rectum fills, excess poop backs up into the rest of the colon and the colon absorbs more water, making the stool harder. In many cases a child's rectum expands so much that it loses its normal tone, like the stretched-out waistband of elastic shorts. The intestine becomes floppy and can't squeeze down effectively to expel the entire load of poop, so some of it stays put in the rectum. And because the intestinal walls have lost elasticity, some of the poop may just fall out. I've seen countless kids who have both urinary problems and poop accidents. One mom told me she'd find "hard little rabbit pellets" all over her house when she would vacuum. When her son, a second grader, would go over to a friend's house, he'd jump on the trampoline and a hard piece of poop would fall out.

Meanwhile, the poop that is building up is located right next to the bladder, squishing it aside. If you've been pregnant (and, admittedly, I haven't, but my wife has given me the play-by-play), you know what it's like to have your bladder encroached upon: You have to pee more often and/or more urgently. Well, what if, instead of a baby, a solid, grapefruit-size mass of poop was pressing on your bladder? Same effect.

The stretching of the colon also can cause the nerves that control the bladder to go haywire, making the bladder hiccup like crazy. The result: wet underwear, during the day or overnight. (I explain this phenomenon in detail in Chapter 3.) Less commonly the opposite happens: The bladder becomes under-active. The child can't pee because the stretched-out rectum has turned off nerve stimulation to the bladder and/or impinged upon and obstructed the bladder neck. A related problem is urinary tract infection (UTI). As I explain in Chapter 4, stock-piling trillions of bacteria in that big pile of poop so close to the bladder opening makes infection in girls almost inevitable. Even once constipation has been treated, the nerves feeding the bladder may not quiet down right away. Nerve irritation often persists for months. Of course some kids luck out and their bladders aren't affected by constipation, which explains why not all kids with constipation have urinary problems.

Unclogging Your Child's Colon

Children of all ages come to our clinic with urinary prob-lems such as accidents, bedwetting, UTIs, urgency and fre-quency problems, and painful peeing. Whether a child has one of these issues or several, relieving the poop burden in his rectum is the single most effective therapy. Incidentally, getting your child unclogged also will relieve symptoms of constipation that are unrelated to the bladder, such as chronic abdominal pain and poor appetite. Despite the perception that children outgrow constipation, research shows that among kids who are chronically stopped up, some 30 percent and probably more, according to my gastroenterologist colleagues, will remain constipated into the teenage years and adulthood. Even if your child outgrows the accidents and bedwetting, he may face a lifetime of discomfort and inconvenience. So for all kinds of reasons, it's critical to resolve constipation sooner rather than later.

So how do you start? For virtually all of my patients I begin with a full-on intestinal clean out, typically using a high dose of laxatives, and sometimes enemas and other measures. (This is done on a weekend so the child isn't leaking poop at school.) Almost invariably these children's problems are caused by a poop mass in the rectum, and as long as the mass remains, the problems won't resolve. Timid measures won't cut it. After the colon gets clear, we move onto the maintenance phase. This involves three strategies: a lower dose laxative regimen for six months, a higher fiber diet (see Chapter 8), and healthier pooping habits (see "Helping Your Child Become a Super Pooper" on page 60 and Chapter 9, which includes physical therapy techniques). Of course before you adopt any of these therapies, clear the plan with your pediatrician.

Why It's Okay to Give Children Laxatives

Yes, you read that correctly: I recommend laxatives for children, first in high doses and then in lower doses for months, sometimes years. Perhaps you are thinking: *Hold on just a moment—isn't it unsafe to give laxatives to a two-year-old? Aren't they addictive?* That depends on what kind of laxative you give a child. But in general, laxatives are an important part of treating constipation, because, simply put, they work, they work quickly, and they're safe.

A high-fiber diet, while important for preventing a constipation relapse, can take a while to implement, especially if a child has been staging a lifelong vegetable strike. Even if you get your kid munching on carrots and eating her PB&J on whole-wheat bread, it can take a few weeks for her bowels to adjust. And anyway, all of the roughage in the supermarket isn't going to dislodge a softball-size mass of poop stuck in a child's rectum. Similarly, persuading a reluctant child to sit on the potty for five minutes twice a day can take a lot of work, or bribery, on a parent's part, and, truth be told, good potty habits aren't enough to get a seriously constipated child cleaned out.

Some parents resist using laxatives because they feel this isn't a "natural" approach. My response is this: Carrying around a colon full of poop throughout a kid's entire childhood, a common scenario these days, is not natural either. Also not natural: walking around with a tube inserted through your abdomen into your colon so you can flush out poop with liquid laxatives. Yet that scenario, known as a cecostomy, is becoming more common in children whose severe constipation has gone untreated for years. Getting your kid cleaned out is critical, and more often than not, laxatives are the most effective approach. As one of my colleagues, a pediatric gastroenterologist, told me, "Parents are terrified of the consequences of giving their kids laxatives, but what about the consequences of taking out part of a six-year-old's colon? Many people don't realize how severe the cost of undermanagement can be." This doctor has performed more than one hundred cecostomies in children whose stretched-out colons are permanently damaged from constipation and has sent more than a handful of his worst-case patients to surgeons for colostomies.

To be clear: Not all laxatives are the same. The laxatives some folks have a notion to avoid, and in some cases for good reason, are stimulant laxatives such as Ex-Lax. These medications, which come in over-the-counter or prescription form, stimulate the intestinal muscles to contract and squeeze out the idle poop.

Stimulant laxatives can be habit-forming in high doses over extended periods, so it is best that pediatric gastroenterologists rather than pediatricians or urologists prescribe them. But when a child's rectum has been stretched over a period of years, stimulant laxatives may be necessary for a few months, perhaps longer, to restore normal bowel motility. An experienced pediatric gastroenterologist will make sure your child does not take too much of this medication or take it for too long.

Osmotic laxatives—you probably know them as Mira-LAX or generic versions—are a different story. These over-the-counter powders draw water into the colon so the poop stays soft, much like dietary fiber but far more effectively for significant cases of constipation. The key ingredient is PEG 3350, polyethylene glycol, which is safe for long-term use and is not habit-forming. It's also easy to give to kids because it has no taste or odor; you can mix it in their beverages, and they typically won't complain. These laxatives have virtually no downside, other than the remote possibility of dehydration with overuse. But you'd notice diarrhea and cut back on these laxatives long before your child would become dehydrated.

You may search the shelves at the store for a children's version of MiraLAX only to come up empty. The reason: PEG 3350 is not approved by the U.S. Food and Drug Administration (FDA) for use in children. So now you're thinking: *What???! Is this idiot doctor recommending I give my children a medicine that the government has not even determined is safe in children?* That was precisely my wife's reaction when I suggested we give Mira-LAX to our oldest (and clearly constipated) daughter, complete with the "idiot doctor" terminology. It's a reaction I get daily, and understandably, from conscientious parents. So let me explain.

The reason PEG 3350 has not been approved by the FDA for use in children is *not* because studies show it is unsafe in children. In fact more than one hundred studies of PEG 3350 have been conducted in children, and none of these studies suggests the substance is harmful. Most of these studies have been published in well-respected, peer-reviewed journals, and they show quite clearly that long-term use of PEG 3350 is not only effective and safe in children but virtually free of significant side effects. The side effects that have turned up are rare and include flatulence, nausea, abdominal cramping, and vomiting.[9] (By the way, I have never had any parent report that his child vomited after using PEG 3350.)

Not only has MiraLAX been shown to be safe in children and toddlers, but a study published in one of the American Academy of Pediatrics' own journals[10] demonstrated that PEG 3350 can be used safely for months in children younger than eighteen

9   www.ncbi.nlm.nih.gov/pmc/articles/PMC2682301/.
10   AAP Grand Rounds.

months old, with no systemic absorption. In other words, the stuff never actually gets into the child's bloodstream; it just washes out the colon. The intestines are designed for absorption, somewhat like a filter, so the fear with any ingested drug is how much gets absorbed and how that absorbed drug may affect the body. PEG 3350 is great because it just sits in the intestine, and then you poop it out. What's more, PEG 3350 appears to have no effect on the body's balance of electrolytes (potassium, sodium, and other substances essential for the body's cells and organs to function), so this laxative can be used long-term.

MiraLAX and its generic cousins are recommended by the major medical associations involved in pediatric care. In reference to pediatric gastrointestinal problems, the American Academy of Gastroenterology states that PEG 3350 is "safe and non-habit forming." The College of Family Physicians of Canada considers PEG 3350 to be "a safe, effective, and well-tolerated option for treatment of constipation in children," even for kids younger than two years of age.[11]

If the fact that two of my own children take MiraLAX daily and that pretty much every pediatrician, pediatric urologist, and pediatric gastroenterologist in North America uses PEG 3350 as the main treatment for constipation isn't enough to persuade you this stuff is okay, try this: When the *Pediatric Journal of Gastroenterology and Nutrition* published the Recommendations of the North American Society of Pediatric Gastroenterology, Hepatology, and Nutrition for the treatment of constipation in

---

11   Chung S, Chung R, Goldman R. Polyethylene glycol 3350 without electrolytes for treatment of childhood constipation. *Can Fam Physician.* May 2009; 55(5):481-82.

children, guess what was one of the first-line treatments they recommended? You guessed it: PEG 3350. The American Academy of Pediatrics endorses this recommendation.[12]

So why hasn't PEG 3350 been approved for use in children? Because it costs a boatload of money to conduct the necessary studies to achieve FDA approval. A company could have a million independent studies conducted on children, but if they were not studies designed and approved by the FDA—a complex, lengthy, and expensive process—the company cannot use the evidence to make a case for FDA approval. PEG 3350 is available over the counter and is taken by children all over the world every day, so Merck & Co., the manufacturer of MiraLAX, simply has no incentive to pay the FDA gobs of money to prove something that everyone already knows.

Once the FDA approves a drug for any indicated use, physicians may legally prescribe the drug for patients in other age groups. That's called "off-label" use, and it's common practice. In fact, here's a statistic that may surprise you: Nearly 80 percent of children receive off-label medications during hospitalizations. The reality is, only a small number of drugs have been formally tested in children.[13] Because PEG 3350 is actually one of them, I feel no qualms about recommending it to parents.

At the same time, I don't insist that my patients take MiraLAX. I don't care what you use to get your child's rectum empty. I just want it empty! In fact, if you really want to attack the

---

12 http://aappolicy.aappublications.org/misc/Constipation_in_Infants_and_Children.dtl.

13 Shah SS, Hall M, et al. Off-label drug use in hospitalized children. *Arch Pediatr Adolesc Med.* Mar 2007; 161(3):282–90.

problem head on, you may want to bypass PEG 3350 and follow the program that Dr. Sean O'Regan, introduced in Chapter 1, used on his five-year-old son and on the hundreds of Canadian patients he studied: a daily Fleet enema for a month, an enema every other day for a second month, and then twice a week for the third month. If you use enemas (clean outs from the bottom up using a bottle or bag of saline solution with a nozzle), I guarantee your child's rectum will be clean and that any constipation-related bladder problems will resolve.

There's a funny thing about putting stuff in people's bottoms, though: They don't like it. Dr. O'Regan told me that his son never complained about the enemas and neither did any of his patients or their parents. But that has not been my experience, at least for school-age children. While preschoolers tend not to protest, older kids seem to find the process uncomfortable and embarrassing. To most people the bottom is off-limits (exit only!). Also, compared to mixing a powder in water, enemas aren't a great long-term solution. Keeping a child's colon clear is an ongoing process, one that can last many months, even years, so osmotic laxatives are particularly well suited for the job.

In addition to enemas, there are plenty of other laxatives designed for children, and I discuss many of them in the sidebar "More Help for Unclogging Your Child's Colon" on page 56. Also, some kids, for reasons unknown, respond better to an osmotic laxative called lactulose than they do to PEG 3350. Lactulose, a sweet, syrupy liquid, is available only by prescription. But in my experience, PEG 3350 works best for most kids and keeps parents happy because it doesn't involve shoving anything up their children's bottoms.

Clean-Outs for Severe Constipation

If you picked up this book because your child is having wet-ting problems, poop accidents, episodes of frequent or pain-ful peeing, or recurrent UTIs, you can be pretty sure she needs the Rocket Rooter treatment before going on the maintenance therapy described in the next section. (To be absolutely sure, I recommend getting her X-rayed.) The method of choice for

HOW TO GET YOUR KID UNCLOGGED ASAP

Here's the laxative clean-out regimen we typically use at my clinic. Ask your doctor if it's appropriate for your child.

• *Initial clean out:* Start this process on a Friday night, so you have the entire weekend to get the job done. For children lighter than about forty-five pounds, mix seven doses of MiraLAX or generic-brand powder (one dose is a cap filled to the line) in 32 ounces of Gatorade, Pedialyte, or other clear, noncarbonated liquid. Gatorade and Pedialyte help prevent dehydration because they contain electrolytes. Plus, they taste good, so kids may be more motivated to drink the full dose. Have your child drink the entire bottle over twenty-four hours. She can eat anything she wants but should drink only this fluid.

Kids weighing between forty-five and eighty pounds should get about ten doses, and those weighing at least eighty pounds should receive fourteen doses of laxative in 64 ounces of fluid for the first twenty-four hours. Don't give her less than this amount! You may even need to give her more. The endpoint you're shooting for is watery poop. Your child most families is a large dose of osmotic laxative, which flushes out the colon from the top down. Anyone who has ever had a colonoscopy knows the drill. In many cases, a supermega dose of PEG 3350 is enough to break apart and dislodge the clog. (See the sidebar, "How to Get Your Kid Unclogged ASAP" on page 54 for details.) Just beware! Clean-outs are a mess, which is why I recommend starting on a weekend and having your

should pass five or six stools within twenty-four to forty-eight hours. If she doesn't, keep her on the maintenance dose described below and try the initial clean-out program again the next weekend, keeping her on a daily capful of MiraLAX during the week.

- *Maintenance:* Following the bowel clearing, give your child one cap of the laxative in 8 ounces of fluid daily, and have her sit on the toilet after all meals, especially breakfast, using a footstool for support if necessary. She also should blow out while pooping, which will help her bottom muscles relax.

- *Weaning from laxatives:* When your child's constipation has been fully resolved for six months, gradually lower the dose of MiraLAX. First, cut the dose in half for two weeks. Then give her half a dose every other day for two weeks, and then every third day for two weeks. Then stop. If at any time your child seems backed up again, simply revert one step. About 50 percent of kids will relapse after the first attempted weaning. Parents often mistake this for addiction to or dependence on the MiraLAX, but that's not the case. Holding poop is just a tough habit to break. Wait another month or so and try again.

child stay near a toilet She may even need pull-ups during this treatment, because she might have poop accidents or end up with diarrhea that leaks out.

Some parents, fearful of a possible gush of diarrhea, attempt to clean out their child's colon using a daily small dose of Mira-LAX. This almost never works. To see improvement your child's rectum needs to retract to normal size, and that won't happen

MORE HELP FOR UNCLOGGING YOUR CHILD'S COLON

Not every child has success with or is willing to drink a fluid mixed with PEG 3350. (Some kids swear they can taste it and don't like it.) Different strategies are effective for different kids, and sometimes a combination of products and procedures works best for resolving a clogged rectum. Here are some options to consider in addition to PEG 3350 and lactulose.

• *Pedia-Lax chewable tablets.* These watermelon-flavored tablets, which taste like candy, are essentially a children's dose of Milk of Magnesia, a type of osmotic laxative. They work by increasing water content in poop. The child must drink a glass of water with each tablet. Be sure to follow the directions on the bottle so your child doesn't consume too many and wind up with massive diarrhea.

• *Glycerin suppositories in solid form.* Glycerin suppositories are small, gel-like bullets that you insert in the child's bottom. They pull water from the colon, softening the hardened poop, and also stimulate movement in the rectum muscles, helping lure the poop out, often within minutes. Pedia-Lax also makes liquid until the clump of poop dissipates. A few doses of MiraLAX are unlikely to break apart a solid mass that has been irritating your child's bladder for months or years.

Within twenty-four to forty-eight hours of starting the clean out, your child should pass five or six stools. Don't be surprised if it takes multiple clean-outs to get his colon unblocked. The best way to figure out whether your child's colon has been

glycerin suppositories that come with a mess-free applicator and may work more quickly than the solid suppositories.

- *Ex-Lax.* Under the direction of a pediatric gastroenterologist, stimulant laxatives can be a very effective way of eliminating a poop mass, getting a child's bowels moving again, and returning a stretched-out rectum to normal size. Adding stimulant laxatives tends to do the job more quickly than osmotic laxatives alone.

- *Enema.* The smartest person I know, Dr. Sean O'Regan, the doctor whose research proved everything I believe about childhood urinary problems, used enema therapy with dramatic success. Unlike osmotic laxatives, enemas get right at the problem and provide immediate results.

- *Hospital clean-out.* If your child is experiencing severe abdominal pain and can't pee—because his bladder neck has been so squished or because the muscles of the bladder wall are so stretched that they can't push out urine—your doctor may admit your child to the hospital for a procedure that involves placing a tube through his nose and down into his stomach. The doctor starts pumping in laxative, and eventually, the poop starts flowing. This is truly a last resort.

cleared is a follow-up X-ray. If forty-eight hours pass and all is silent, try some of the products described in the "More Help for Unclogging Your Child's Colon" sidebar on page 56.

Despite the mess, most kids are so happy to find relief that the process isn't a bother. Even if a child hasn't complained about constipation, she may know intuitively that something is wrong and be eager to go along with the program. If the process upsets your child, reassure her that none of this is her fault, and it's simply what the doctor recommended to help her feel better.

Some kids, however, are so clogged up that they need extreme amounts of osmotic laxative to get the job done, and trying to wash out the entire colon to get to the clog at the end is both overkill and ineffective. PEG 3350 may cause such a rapid rush of liquid out the rectum that it simply bypasses the hard poop mass, leaving the lump intact. Because of the mess, parents may stop short of the full clean-out process and assume prematurely, and without getting follow-up X-rays, that the child's colon is clear.

In cases where you feel MiraLAX isn't working for your child—either because the diarrhea is too overwhelming or the symptoms aren't improving—you may need to add a stimulant laxative such as Ex-Lax under the supervision of a gastroen-terologist, or use daily enemas, such as the Fleet enema by Pedia-Lax, with the guidance of a gastroenterologist or pedia-trician. Honestly, if every family would agree to the enema regimen, that would be my first choice for severely consti-pated children.

Post–Clean-Out Maintenance Regimen

Once your child is unclogged, she should stay on an osmotic laxative until her problems have been resolved for a full six months. That's also an appropriate length of time for a child as young as age one who hasn't (yet) developed urinary problems but who displays some of the signs of constipation listed earlier in this chapter, such as chronically firm or large poops. (The rare infant who has hard, infrequent poops likely has intestinal problems and requires a workup by a pediatric gastroenterologist.) I've never seen a parent keep her child on laxatives too long. Stopping too soon is typically the problem, so keep an open-door policy with regard to your child and the bathroom. Only when you stay involved can you judge if and when you can stop the laxatives.

Typically a half a cap of laxative once a day is a good starting dose for young kids. That's 8 ½ grams, mixed in water, juice, milk, or any other noncarbonated beverage. PEG 3350 dissolves best in clear liquids and poorly in carbonated drinks. If you put it in milk, stir vigorously; otherwise, it'll form lumps and sink to the bottom. (If your child likes smoothies, you can get away with calling the lumpy goop the "smoothie part" and he may well drink it.) Some children need a full cap daily. Some kids poop pellets even on that dose and need even more.

The great thing about osmotic laxatives is that you can't mess up the dose. If you give your child too much, she'll have diarrhea, so you'll know instantly to back off. If you don't give her enough laxative, her poop stays hard. Finding that sweet spot may take some trial and error, but ultimately it shouldn't be difficult.

The biggest mistake parents make is using laxatives inconsistently, causing their child to swing between very firm and very loose poops. Children who regularly poop marbles or logs are better off remaining on a low dose daily until the problems that started the therapy have resolved for six months than taking large doses every time painful poops begin.

Even if MiraLAX works miracles for your child, be sure to work on improving his eating habits. A fiber-rich diet is essential to keeping him free of constipation in the long run. If you're having trouble coaxing him into eating more fruits, veggies, whole grains, and beans, he may benefit from a fiber supplement such as Benefiber, which easily dissolves in liquids, or fiber gummies (look for brands with 3 grams of fiber per gummy.) But fiber supplements are no substitute, nutritionwise, for actual food. Constipated children also should drink plenty of fluids, which help keep their poop from drying out, and should get out to play as much as possible. As I explain in Chapter 9, physical activity helps keep things moving.

Helping Your Child Become a Super Pooper

Laxatives and fiber, along with water and physical activity, will go a long way toward relieving constipation and preventing a relapse, but to stay unclogged for the long haul, kids also need to develop healthy pooping habits. They are, after all, going to be pooping for the rest of their lives. Since children are naturally averse to interrupting their days to take a trip to the toilet, they need to perceive pooping as a nonnegotiable part of their daily routine, like picking up their dirty clothes and brushing their teeth. Ultimately they need to learn to go as soon as they get the urge, but first things first: They need to be instructed to sit on the toilet regularly. Here's what I suggest:

- *Have your child try to poop after breakfast and dinner.* You may have discovered from personal experience that there is a reflex emptying of the bowels after you've eaten, and this urge, called the gastrocolic reflex, is strongest in the morning. Also, pooping in the morning prevents a child from holding it at school. Make sure her feet are well supported as she sits on the toilet. She'll probably need a stool to rest her feet on. Even if your child poops after breakfast, have her try again after dinner. Parents often are amazed at how much poop their child can produce when asked!

- *Instruct your child to sit for a full five minutes.* Often kids will pop off the potty after ten seconds and claim they don't have to poop. But if you insist that they give it a full five minutes, they may become poop machines. Try an oven timer or a five-minute sand timer. If necessary, bribe your child with stickers or toys. Just don't offer him potato chips.

- *Encourage your child to relax her bottom while she's on the toilet.* Since reading the *Wall Street Journal* probably won't work, have her bring a favorite book or toy. Ideally, she'll become so distracted that she won't tense up. Blowing into her hands or into a balloon also helps. The idea is to force her to strain with her abdominal muscles so she can't clench her sphincter. Chapter 9 offers several techniques to help a child relax on the potty.

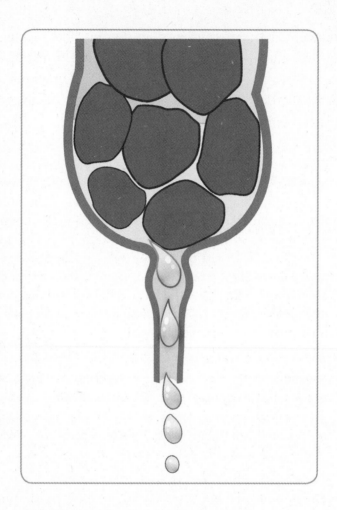

Figure 2-2
Sometimes kids appear to have diarrhea when they actually are constipated. That's because when a large, hard stool is clogging the rectum, as in this diagram, loose poop can ooze by and find a way out more easily than the hard stuff.

Patience! Patience!

If you've been dealing with your child's wetting problems for quite some time, you're probably relieved to find out their cause and eager to get these issues fixed. But please, temper your expectations! Some kids do see remarkable results—I've had preteen patients who wet their beds their entire lives be cured of the problem within a week simply by taking MiraLAX. But that's not the norm. And the quick results that Dr. O'Regan got—remember the children in Chapter 1 whose bedwetting problems were cured on average in sixteen days?—are likely a best-case scenario because the daily enema therapy he prescribed is more aggressive (and less palatable to most families) than laxative therapy.

Even with laxatives and the world's healthiest diet, constipation problems in kids can take months, sometimes years, to fix. Holding habits die hard. Most often the problem doesn't resolve completely until the child becomes comfortable pooping any time and anywhere she needs to go. This may not happen until adulthood, and sometimes never happens (you know who you are!). In rare cases, children with severe, chronic constipation require surgery to insert a tube into the colon—the cecostomy I mentioned earlier in this chapter. Once a day the child places a catheter in the tube and pours in about a gallon of saline solution to flush out the colon.

But that's the worst-case scenario. Most children can avoid drastic measures by following the steps I've outlined here. My best advice to Mom and Dad: Stay involved. I know most parents dream of the day when they can be completely removed from their children's goings-on in the bathroom. Heck, I look forward to that day myself. But don't get too fixated on your own potty liberation. You need to pay attention to your kids' pooping habits until it becomes uncomfortable for both of you, which may well be puberty.

CHAPTER 3

Overcoming Accidents

A mom recently came to my clinic with her five-year-old daughter convinced that the girl had become diabetic. "She'll pee in the toilet, and then five minutes later she'll have an accident," the mom said, clearly stressed out. "Then she'll pee five more times in an hour. Isn't excessive peeing a sign of diabetes?"

Yes, it can be, along with unquenchable thirst, weight loss, weakness, and fatigue. But this woman's daughter—rosy cheeks, all smiles, plenty of energy to jump on and off my exam table ten times—was the picture of health.

The mom went on to describe her daughter's potty history: She'd trained at twenty-two months with virtually no instruction and was a toileting rock star until age three and a half, when she began rushing to the bathroom. "We didn't think much of it," the mom recalled. "You know how kids are. They get caught up in playing or watching TV and wait too long." By age five, the girl wasn't making it to the bathroom on time. Sometimes she wouldn't mention her accidents until Mom or Dad asked about her wet clothes. "It's like she can't even feel it when she goes," the mom said.

I ran a urine test on the girl, to rule out diabetes and reassure her mom. I do this all the time. I've met with hundreds of parents who are sure their child has diabetes. Here's how many tests have come back positive: none. Only once in my career have I encountered a patient with wetting problems who had a serious medical condition, a twelve-year-old boy who had a malformation in his urethra.

In virtually all cases one of three scenarios (or often a combination) is at play:

- The child is constipated, and the large poop load is crowding out or irritating her bladder.
- The child has been chronically holding her pee, causing her bladder to thicken and become hyperactive.
- The child pees with her legs together, forcing some urine into her vagina, only to drip out later.

This chapter helps you pinpoint the causes of your child's wake-time accidents and put a stop to them. (Chapter 4 covers bedwetting during sleep, which is a different, though often related, issue.) In most cases the problems underlying accidents can be solved in a matter of months, as children's bodies are resilient, but do note that daytime accidents tend to take longer to resolve than bedwetting and other urinary problems. Bedwetting, along with frequent or urgent peeing, are early warning signs of bladder overactivity, but by the time a child is wetting while awake, the bladder has developed more significant problems. What's important is addressing them now so your child's condition doesn't linger into adolescence and adulthood and develop into a more serious problem (as sometimes it can), such as pelvic pain or pain with sexual intercourse. And, of course, the sooner you solve the issues, the sooner you can ease your family's stress level and lighten your laundry basket.

Nope, Accidents Aren't Normal

Given how many potty-trained kids have accidents, it's no wonder parents get the impression that wetting, like throwing temper tantrums, is just something kids do. But accidents aren't normal. Potty-trained kids, no matter how deeply involved in their Xbox or sandbox, shouldn't have accidents any more often than adults do. In truth the only time when it actually *is* natural for a child to wet himself is when he's first learning to use the toilet.

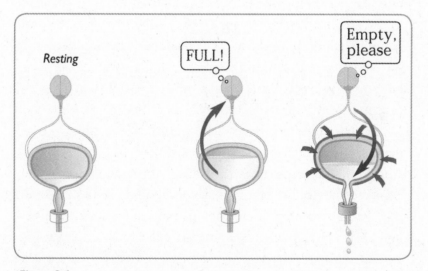

Figure 3-1
In babies, voiding happens by reflex: A full bladder sends a signal to the spinal cord, triggering automatic bladder emptying.

During this transition period a lot is happening in a child's brain. As you can see in Figure 3-1, your brain and bladder are connected by nerves that are housed in, and sprout from, the spinal cord. In adults, and anyone who is toilet trained, the brain controls the bladder. When your bladder is full, your brain receives the signal that it's time to head to the bathroom and then signals your bladder to release pee. It's pretty straightforward.

But in babies, that signal from the bladder never reaches the brain. As a baby's bladder fills, a signal travels to the spinal cord, a reflex signal comes right back to the bladder, and the baby pees. The great thing about babies is that they don't think about peeing; they just go. Although parents often are in a hurry to get their children out of diapers, as a urologist I love to see kids in diapers, because this is when their peeing and pooping habits are healthiest. The bladder does exactly what it was designed to do: fill and empty of urine regularly. Nobody is holding the bladder back, waiting until he is done playing with his toys, or until he can get to a clean bathroom.

When children learn to use the toilet, two main things happen (in addition to parental celebrating and shopping for Elmo or Dora underwear). First, kids become aware of the urge and the need to empty their bowels and bladder. Second, they learn to control when they pee by squeezing and relaxing the urethral sphincter, a small circular muscle that wraps around the urethra (the tube you pee out of). The rectum has its own separate sphincter that works the same way. In other words the process is no longer confined to the spinal cord reflex. The brain gets involved, and for young kids, that's nothing but trouble.

> **Myth:** *Holding urine helps build bladder capacity.*
>
> **Fact:** *Regular peeing makes a child's bladder grow. Studies show that the bladder needs to cycle to grow; in other words, it needs to fill enough that the walls stretch a bit and then empty completely under low pressure.*

Now, the child has to sense that her bladder is full, decide that she wants to go, and find a comfortable and safe place to relieve herself. Then she needs to go there, relax her sphincter, and take the time to actively and completely empty her bladder. That's a lot to ask of a two-year-old! So as you can imagine, in kids who are potty trained at a young age, there's a greater chance that things will go awry. That's why I don't recommend toilet training before age three or thereabouts. But even children trained at age three or older can have accidents for the reasons described in the next two sections.

All children are different, so the time it takes a child to make the new brain-bladder connection varies greatly, from a couple days to several months. During this time your child is apt to have his share of accidents, especially if this period coincides with the start of preschool or another major life change. That said, most kids train quickly, and those who take several months to train or never seem to finish training, typically have an underlying reason for the delay, such as constipation. Once a child is trained, he's all set and shouldn't have accidents, no matter how busy he is. So why, then, do so many potty-trained kids wet their pants?

The Number One Cause of Accidents: Constipation

When kids are constipated—and almost all children who have accidents are—they walk around with intestines that are full of poop. As I explain in gory detail in Chapter 2, much of this poop sits in the pelvis, right behind the bladder. Since there is only so much room in the pelvis, the bladder gets squeezed out of the way and, as a result, is able to hold less urine. Also, the nerves controlling the bladder, which run between the bladder and the intestines, can get irritated when the intestines are enlarged, causing unexpected and unwanted bladder contractions—in other words: mad dashes to the toilet and accidents.

Most parents of constipated children don't realize their children are backed up, because most of these kids still poop regularly. But it's actually the size and shape of poop that best indicates whether a child is carrying around a load in his intestines. Chapter 2 includes a section titled "Eleven Signs Your Child Is Constipated," which will help you determine if constipation is a problem for your child. If you're unsure or want an idea of just how clogged up your child's insides are, I recommend getting your child X-rayed. Chapter 2 explains more about abdominal X-rays and covers the various therapies for constipation, but to recap, here are the key points. I can't emphasize enough how important it is to treat constipation promptly and aggressively.

- *Add polyethylene glycol powder—MiraLAX or its generic equivalent—to your child's diet.* This laxative powder has no taste and can be mixed into water, milk, or any other noncarbonated liquid. Use as much as is it takes to get the child's poop to the consistency of a thick milk shake or pudding, usually about a capful, or 17 grams. This type of laxative is completely safe long-term (unlike stimulant laxatives such as Ex-Lax), so keep your child on it until her potty problems have been completely resolved for six months. If your child needs to take MiraLAX for years, that's fine!

- *Increase your child's fiber intake to 14 to 31 grams a day, depending on his age.* (See the chart in Chapter 8.) This isn't difficult, but if your child is low on fiber—and 88 percent of children are—increasing her intake may require some research and experimentation on your part. Chapter 8 lists plenty of kid-friendly foods that are rich in fiber and provides tips on getting your child to eat more fruits, veggies, whole grains, and beans.

- *Every day, have your child sit on the toilet and try to poop for at least five minutes after breakfast and dinner.* There's a reflex for emptying of the bowels following stomach filling, and this reflex is strongest in the morning. Also, pooping first thing in the morning at home prevents a child from holding poop at school.

With constipation successfully treated, many children stop having accidents within weeks or months without trying any other strategies. If you are certain that your child is cleared up and yet he continues to wet after three months, he probably has a severely thickened bladder from holding his pee, so you'll need to continue bladder retraining with a timed peeing schedule and possibly bladder-relaxing medication, as I explain in the next section.

The Number Two Reason Kids Have Accidents: Chronic Holding

Children essentially become toilet trained once they learn to hold or delay pooping and peeing, by squeezing either sphincter muscle. This squeezing sends a signal to the spinal cord to stop the contraction of the bowel or bladder and puts off the urge to go for a while. Most adults do this only when we absolutely need to, like when we're in a car or stuck in a store without a bathroom.

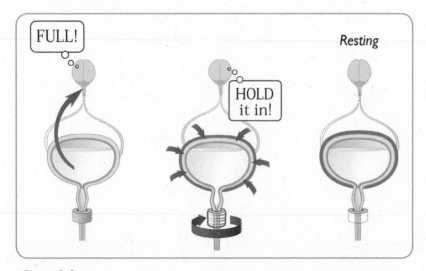

Figure 3-2
When children are toilet trained, they develop the ability to hold pee by squeezing the urethral sphincter, causing bladder contractions to stop.

But kids hold their pee all the time. That's because children—and I mean *all* children—don't like going to the bathroom. They would rather play, watch TV, even clean their rooms than interrupt their lives to eliminate bodily fluids. What's more, kids often aren't in charge of their schedules, so even if they want to go they may not be able to (for example, during school). Once they learn to put off peeing, children tend to do so as long as they can. We've all seen kids delay going to the bathroom. We even have a name for it: the "potty dance," an elaborate number involving squirming, curtseying, or crotch grabbing.

You might have heard that holding pee is a good thing—that it helps stretch kids' bladders so they can hold more urine, thereby eliminating accidents. Even some pediatricians recommend that kids who pee too frequently increase the time between trips to the toilet so that they can learn to hold more pee. But this is poor advice! Regular emptying is actually what leads to healthy bladder growth; holding urine, on the other hand, leads to smaller bladder capacity and sets a child up for accidents.

Why Holding Pee Leads to Accidents

The bladder is basically a bag—in the size range of a grapefruit to a cantaloupe, depending on a person's age—designed to hold pee. The outlet through which this bag empties, known as the bladder neck, is always closed, except when you're peeing. The bladder neck remains closed without any effort on your part.

But the bladder is not just a bag; it's a muscular bag. When it isn't storing urine, it's squeezing to empty that urine out. Every time you feel the urge to pee, you are feeling your bladder begin to squeeze and your bladder neck open up a bit. But squeezing the sphincter keeps you from wetting and signals to the bladder to stop squeezing. The sphincter is saying, "Not now, hold on a bit," and the urge goes away. We all do this once in a while, and it is completely normal, not to mention necessary, in a decent society. You can't pee just anywhere!

The problem is that each time you squeeze your sphincter to override your bladder's squeezing and prevent the release of pee, you create resistance that strains your bladder. What happens when muscles go up against resistance? Exactly what happens when you train your hamstrings at the gym: They get thicker and stronger. Essentially the sphincter is engaged in a tug-of-war against the bladder: One (the bladder) is trying to empty by squeezing to expel urine, while the other (the sphincter) is trying to hold the urine in by compressing the opening of the bladder. When the sphincter wins, you are dry; when the bladder wins, you're wet.

The sphincter always starts off stronger. That's the only way anyone could stay dry. The few times a day that we adults need to hold our pee doesn't lead to any appreciable change in the bladder muscle. But when a child consistently delays peeing, over months and years, his bladder wall becomes thicker and more muscular. As a result, his bladder capacity decreases and his bladder contracts more forcefully. A good analogy is a balloon. You know how a thin-walled, stretched-out balloon is

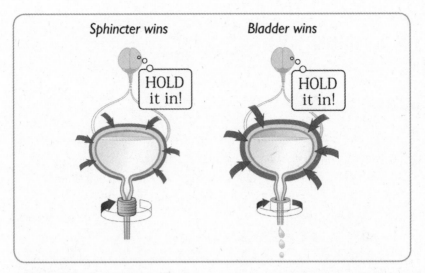

Figure 3-3
In a child who chronically holds pee, the bladder thickens and overpowers the sphincter, leading to wetting.

easy to blow up? Now picture a balloon made of really thick rubber. Imagine how hard it would be to blow up and how much force would be necessary to keep it in the air. The same applies to a thick-walled bladder.

To make matters worse, the sensation mechanism of a thick-walled bladder gets out of whack. Your child may get the signal that her bladder is full when it's only partially full. What's more, her bladder starts to have frequent, spontaneous contractions that are more forceful than normal, like hiccups. This is what's happening when your child makes a mad dash to the bathroom.

These sprints are the first sign of the chronic-holding problem. (See sidebar, "Three Signs of Chronic Holding.")

THREE SIGNS OF CHRONIC HOLDING

Chronically holding urine is the root cause of accidents in a large percentage of potty-trained kids. Here are signs that your child is likely a chronic holder:

- *Doing the "potty dance."* Does your son grab at his privates? Does your daughter curtsey and squat on her heels?
- *Mad dashes to the potty.* When your child has to pee, she has to pee *right away*. And she may not always make it to the potty on time.
- *Accidents that seem to come out of the blue.* Your child wets himself with no warning and perhaps without even noticing.

Eventually the bladder gets so strong and irritable that it empties without any input from the child, and the sphincter can't stop the emptying. At this point, which urologists call urge incontinence, kids can't even feel when they need to pee because the bladder squeezes quickly and forcefully and with little warning. About 10 percent of five-year-olds, 5 percent of ten-year-olds, and 1 percent of eighteen-year-olds have urge incontinence. Many more children have urgency without the leakage. All of this is exacerbated by constipation.

Six Solutions for Chronic Holding

To a parent, a child's thickened bladder may sound disconcerting. And indeed, if the problem isn't treated, children can end up with several problems later in life, including, for women, painful sexual intercourse. (See "When Accidents Keep Happening" on page 85.) Fortunately the condition can be reversed by making the bladder thinner and weaker. Anyone who has skipped a few months at the gym is familiar with the best way to sap a muscle's strength: Don't use it. This means making make sure your child's bladder never has to squeeze unless she is actually peeing.

This section includes several strategies to keep your child from holding his pee. Before you implement these strategies, explain them to your child in simple terms. In general these techniques will work best if your child understands them and is willing to cooperate, but too much information may cause stress or confusion. Some children are sick of being wet—it's embarrassing for them, especially at school, and can be quite a psychological burden—and they will gladly cooperate if you just explain that you're starting a program that will help keep them dry. Let your child know the program is not a quick fix but rather requires a long-term commitment.

I believe the persistent "soft sell" works best. Raising your voice while insisting your child go to the bathroom "*RIGHT NOW*" is likely to backfire. "RIGHT NOW or there's no TV" is even less helpful, and expecting rapid improvement will only lead to frustration. On the other hand, reminding your child calmly and matter-of-factly to go regularly and providing positive reinforcement when she does go will help the message sink in. After an accident it may be helpful to remind her, without getting mad or acting frustrated, that she should have gone earlier. The strategies that follow are variations on a simple theme: regular, low-pressure emptying of the bladder. They are complementary, so you can start them all at once.

> **Myth:** *It's normal for potty-trained kids to have accidents when they're distracted.*
>
> **Fact:** *Once they are potty trained, kids shouldn't be any more accident-prone than adults.*

Give your child plenty of fluids to empty.
Keep his bladder on a constant filling/emptying cycle by encouraging him to drink fluids throughout the day. He should drink a few ounces of fluid every few hours so his bladder doesn't fill too quickly (rapid filling can cause overactivity) or stay empty for extended periods of time (a bladder is happiest when it is cycling). Water is best because it's sugar free and has no unwanted side effects on bladder function. In some kids, orange and grapefruit juices cause burning with urination. Avoid giving your child caffeinated beverages, such as caffeinated soda, which can irritate the bladder and make it even more hyperactive. Let your child pick out a special sippy cup that he takes with him wherever he goes, like to the store, on playdates, and to school.

Have your child pee on a schedule, about every two hours.
For kids who don't seem bothered by having accidents, explaining that they need to pee regularly isn't going to help. These kids need a schedule imposed on them. So, send your child to the toilet right before bed, first thing in the morning, and every

two hours throughout the day. To help your child comply while you're not around, and to make the time keeping easier on you, try a children's watch designed to alarm or vibrate every two hours. Search the Internet for "pediatric alarm watch." The best ones allow you to set multiple alarm times so the watch doesn't need to constantly be reset.

If a precise two-hour schedule is unrealistic—for example, if the two-hour mark lands in the middle of tae kwon do class or the bus ride home from school—try a peeing schedule adapted to your child's daily routine. For example, have her use the bathroom right before you leave the house, before snack time, before lunch, after quiet time, and so on. What's important is that your child empties regularly, and *before* she feels the urge to go. Note that many children have such overactive bladders that they cannot go two hours without peeing. These kids may need to take bladder-relaxing medication that only a pediatric urologist can prescribe.

Help your child relax while peeing.

Watch your child as he pees. Does he hold his breath? Is his face turning red? Do his belly muscles seem tight? Kids who hold their urine also tend be constipated, and constipated children have become so used to straining to poop that they think they need to push to pee. They may be so accustomed to holding that they have lost the coordination to relax the urethral sphincter while peeing. Another explanation for the straining, which was proposed by Dr. O'Regan and makes more sense to me, is that carrying around a mass of poop in the rectum has forced the pelvic-floor muscles (described in Chapter 9) into contraction, and even once the stool burden is gone, the muscles may remain tense for a while. For whatever reason, the child ends up peeing through a tight sphincter, which strains the bladder and results in incomplete emptying. A pediatric urologist or physical therapist specializing in potty issues can determine for sure if your child has this problem by having him pee with electrode pads stuck to the area around his bottom; a biofeedback machine will indicate whether his pelvic-floor muscles are relaxing when he pees.

If you notice your child straining, instruct her to breathe deeply and slowly and to keep her belly soft when she pees. Chapter 9 includes tips and exercises that physical therapists use to teach kids how to relax their sphincter as they pee. (Of course, resolving the poop burden in her rectum is job number one.) If your child continues to have trouble, she may benefit from a few sessions with a physical therapist who specializes in this area. Even boys should sit on the toilet, as this encourages them to relax and spend more time trying to pee. If your son absolutely objects to sitting, at least make sure he takes his time; his pants shouldn't go back up as fast as they came down. Kids whose feet dangle in the air when sitting on the toilet need a footstool so they can sit comfortably and avoid straining to keep stable.

Encourage your child to "let it all out."
Many kids let out just enough urine to take away the urge, proclaiming, "All done!" before running off to play. Incomplete emptying leads to frequent urination and sometimes

MEASURING YOUR CHILD'S
BLADDER CAPACITY

You probably know your child's height and weight, but chances are, you have no idea how much pee he can hold. This information can be handy if your child has accidents, wets the bed, or pees too often (more than once every two hours).

If your child's bladder capacity is less than 70 percent of what is expected for a child of her age, she likely has a thickened, hyperactive bladder due to holding, and she may benefit from medication to relax the bladder. Talk to a pediatric urologist about whether this medication, known by the brand names Ditropan and Detrol, is appropriate for your child.

Perform this test only if you are absolutely sure your child's constipation has been cleared up. (In my opinion you need an X-ray to be certain.) Have your child pee into a urine hat, sold at pharmacies, or a homemade urine-collection cup and measuring device. He should do this when he has to pee so badly that he can't hold another drop. Morning is useful because most kids are relatively full right after waking, but the test doesn't have to be done in the morning.

Now, estimate your child's expected bladder capacity using the following formula, which is relatively accurate for children who are at least three years old:

Age + 2, in ounces (1 ounce = 30 ml) = estimated bladder capacity

For example, let's say your child is five years old. Her estimated bladder capacity is 7 ounces (age 5 + 2), or 210 ml. If she peed 126 ml, that's 60 percent of her estimated capacity (126 divided by 210).

wetting and infections. I like to have kids sit for about five minutes at each attempt. The box titled "Getting Your Child to Linger on the Potty" on page 83 offers tips for getting your child to fully empty.

Tell your child when it's time to pee.
When it has been two hours since your child peed or when you see your son grab his privates or your daughter squeeze her legs together, don't ask, "Do you need to go potty?" Children always say no. Instead, offer an instruction: "It's time to go to the bathroom" or "Go potty now, Taylor." If you run into resistance, positive reinforcement helps. For example, promise your child a small reward, such as a sticker, for going. Or, conversely, tell her she can't do whatever fun thing is next—snack, playing, and the like—until she goes. You know your child best; choose whichever strategy you feel is more likely to work.

Be patient.
Some children will sit the entire five minutes and not pee at all, insisting that they absolutely do not need to go, only to get up and pee on the floor minutes later. I know this can be discouraging! But you can only do so much. As long as you put your child on an appropriate schedule and encourage healthy habits, even stubborn kids eventually will catch on. Remember: These habits likely take years for children to develop; you can't reverse them in a week. All you can do is consistently provide the structure and support necessary for good toileting habits, and eventually your child will fall in line.

GETTING YOUR CHILD
TO LINGER ON THE POTTY

Most kids want to hop off the potty ASAP and get back to the fun. There's no simple way to make children empty their bladders when they don't want to, but here are tips for getting your child to sit longer when she insists she is done:

• Have your child count to ten.
• Keep your child's favorite books, puzzles, or toys by the toilet.
• Set a timer for five minutes and tell your child she can get off when the timer rings. Many children respond better to a timer than a parent.
• Put food coloring into the toilet. Kids like watching the pattern changes that urine makes in the water.
• Sprinkle cereal, such as Cheerios, into the toilet to give boys a target.

When Bladder-Relaxing Medication Is Warranted

Many parents ask me to prescribe bladder-relaxing medication to stop their children from having accidents. These meds, known by brand names such as Ditropan and Detrol, are great when used appropriately. But if a child's bladder overactivity is caused by constipation, medicine to calm the bladder will only make things worse. That's because the major side effect of this medication just happens to be . . . constipation. It is important that your child is cleaned out before starting these medications, and the only way to be certain is to have him X-rayed.

If the child's rectum is clear and his bladder is still over-active because its thick walls trigger hiccups, then bladder-relaxing meds typically work well to calm it down, allowing the child to make it to the two-hour peeing intervals that are important for healthy bladder cycling.

Be aware that other side effects can include facial flushing, dry mouth, and blurry vision. But most families I've worked with feel that the benefits outweigh the discomfort to their children, and I try to adjust the dose to achieve maximal benefits with minimal side effects. Children who are good candidates for these medications typically need to stay on them for many months, even years. It often takes that long for the bladder to settle down to its natural state. But they do provide the support necessary to keep the child dry while this process is evolving.

On occasion I prescribe another medical therapy for children with daytime accidents: alpha1-blockers, with brand names such as Flomax and Cardura. These medications, originally designed for men with prostate enlargement, help relax the bladder neck, enabling the bladder to empty at lower pressure. If you lower the dose of these medications, they can be safely used in children, although side effects may include lightheadedness and nasal congestion. I prescribe alpha1-blockers when a regimen of timed peeing and pooping, along with laxatives and possibly Detrol, doesn't do the trick and when testing called flow EMG indicates that the child is unable to relax when peeing. With some kids, peeing frequently isn't enough because they are peeing at high pressure, and this straining contributes to bladder hyperactivity.

WHEN ACCIDENTS KEEP HAPPENING:
THE CONSEQUENCES

Many parents ignore children's problems with toileting because they think accidents are normal, and they assume their kids will grow out of it. And yes, many children do overcome these problems on their own, eventually. But many don't, and I wouldn't recommend waiting to find out which category your child falls into. If dysfunctional elimination is not treated, some of the problems can persist into adulthood and cause painful, lingering conditions related to a chronic inability to relax the pelvic muscles. The possible results of chronic urine holding include the following. (In Chapter 2, I explain the consequences of chronic poop holding.)

- *Pelvic pain syndrome.* In women, this shows up as chronic bladder pain (both when the bladder fills and empties) and in men as either pain with peeing or chronic pain in the area between scrotum and anus. These conditions can be treated, in part, with the pelvic-muscle relaxation exercises discussed in Chapter 9.
- *Pain with sexual intercourse, known as dyspareunia.* This occurs only in women and can be due to an inability to completely relax the pelvic musculature during intercourse. Again this can be treated with pelvic-muscle relaxation techniques.
- *Recurrent urinary tract infections.* At any age, not peeing regularly leads to urine sitting in the bladder for a long time, giving bacteria a chance to grow and causing painful infections. I explain in detail how this happens in Chapter 5.

Ask your pediatric urologist if your child is a good candidate for alpha1-blockers.

Vaginal Voiding: Accidents That Happen Only in Girls

One type of wetting has nothing to do with constipation or waiting too long to pee. It's called vaginal voiding, and (surprise!) it happens only in girls. The most common sign is a small amount of urine spotting in a child's underwear after she has peed. Usually the child can't feel the urine coming out and notices it more often after play or vigorous activity.

Here's what is happening: Little girls tend to pee with their legs close together. When they do this, some of the urine is directed up into the vagina. This urine sits up there until it spills out later with activity. Since the pee isn't coming from the bladder, the child doesn't feel herself wetting but ends up wet all the same.

In girls I examine I often see urine pooled in the vagina. Many girls try to address this problem themselves by stuffing toilet paper in their underwear to keep them dry. Or Mom, not realizing where the urine is coming from, may have her daughter use panty liners to keep her underwear clean.

Vaginal voiding, and the wetting that results from it, is easily treated. Here's what to do:

- *Have your daughter pee with her legs as wide apart as possible.* This position ensures that the urine goes directly from the bladder into the toilet, without touching the skin. If your daughter is wearing pants or tights, she'll probably need to take them all the way off. You can have her try sitting on the toilet backward, which will force her to sit with her legs apart and encourage more urine to go into the toilet. Whatever method you use, make sure your daughter's urine has a direct path to the toilet.

- *Teach your daughter to lean forward to wipe, so any urine that went up into the vagina can drip out.*

- *Have your daughter wipe the inside of her privates when she is done peeing.* Most little girls tend to wipe only the outside, keeping the inner skin (the labia majora) wet.

Think Like a Kid and Other Observations

Treating the problems underlying accidents can be an incredibly frustrating undertaking for parents. In my years of evaluating these kids, I have found that it helps to keep certain things in mind.

First, don't put too much pressure on yourself or your child. All kids will catch on eventually with the right guidance. Just stick with the basic tenets of bowel and bladder therapy and don't push too much, because children often push back.

Myth: Children who have accidents can't feel the urge to pee.

Fact: In children without neurological problems, bladder sensation is always intact. Accidents happen because the bladder has become so overactive that it contracts very forcefully and with little warning.

IS THERE A PSYCHOLOGICAL COMPONENT TO ACCIDENTS?

Some parents are certain that their child is having accidents on purpose, as an act of defiance or a ploy to get attention. Other parents are baffled that their potty-trained child has accidents on their watch but not in front of grandparents or babysitters. So although accidents are almost always the result of chronic holding and/or constipation, in some cases a psychological component may also be involved.

At this point little research has been done on the psychological aspects of wetting. We do know that children who have recently experienced psychological trauma, such as abuse or a stressful divorce, have a higher incidence of both daytime accidents and bedwetting. Situations such as a new sibling or entering a new school may cause a child to regress. We also know that children with Attention-Deficit/Hyperactivity Disorder (ADHD) have ten times the incidence of dysfunctional elimination. This makes a lot of sense, because it takes patience and focus for a child to empty his bladder and bowels on time.

Children who are strong willed or defiant may be more prone to accidents (and more difficult to treat), because they are expressing their independence in one of the few areas of their life that they have complete control over: toileting. Rigid schedules and imposed guidelines often backfire in these children.

If your child is dealing with any of these issues, make sure you are addressing them, possibly with the help of a therapist, at the same time you are working on the therapies described here. I discuss psychological issues in more detail in Chapter 10.

Second, try to think like a kid. I know that it's hard not to become annoyed with your child when he keeps having accidents, especially if he has been potty trained for years. But the reality is some kids may not mind being wet, and that's not so crazy from their perspective. I explain to parents that once the bladder is overactive, it is difficult to control, so the child can't help but wet. Also, something that may be very simple to you—peeing and pooping—may be a stressful or difficult proposition for your child. Maybe this is because he doesn't have access to safe, clean toilets at school or simply because it's the last thing on his mind.

Finally, keep in mind that all human decisions, to some extent, are based on gaining some benefit and/or avoiding pain. Your child may hold her poop, for example, because of a painful episode of constipation in the past. I'm in favor of anything you can do to limit the pain children associate with toileting—for example, by keeping her poop soft—or to increase the benefit she gains by going, such as offering a reward. This is one instance where I'm all in favor of bribery!

CHAPTER 4

Bedwetting:
Helping Your Child Stay Dry All Night

When you're caring for a baby, sleep deprivation comes with the territory, but you don't expect your first grader to venture into your room night after night and announce, "Mom, my bed is wet." In the scramble to find fresh sheets while your child changes into clean pjs, you're probably thinking: *Is this some weird stage, or is something wrong?* The older your child is, the more likely he's wondering the same thing, especially if he's worried about going on sleepovers or camping trips.

In this chapter I explain how to gauge whether your child's bedwetting warrants treatment and which therapies work best. My take on this topic is a bit different from what you may hear from other physicians. Most doctors won't treat bedwetting in kids under age seven, because it's so common and because most kids do outgrow it. True enough. But in my experience many cases of bedwetting that appear to be normal and not worth treating actually have underlying causes that can be dealt with fairly easily, almost always without medication. In short, many families with young kids are suffering when they don't need to be.

The same goes for older kids, too. Often there's a quick, drug-free fix for tween and teen bed wetters, even those who have been peeing in their sleep for years. In other cases there's a slower but almost certain solution. With treatment the outlook for bed wetters of all ages is invariably good. Without therapy many childhood bed wetters grow into college kids who have to deal with that stress on top of their midterms. That's right—up to 2.5 percent of college kids regularly wet their beds. The remedies in this chapter should ensure that your child is not among them.

Bedwetting: When It's Normal, When It's Not

Bedwetting is typically a developmental issue. In other words, young kids pee when they sleep, and grown-ups don't, and at some point in between—when our bladders are large enough and brains mature enough—all of us gain the ability, subconsciously, to keep ourselves dry at night. As with all other developmental milestones, such as walking, talking, and complaining about their bedtime, some kids reach this stage earlier or later than others do. At age three, about 50 percent of kids pee in their sleep. By age five, about 10 to 20 percent aren't yet reliably dry.

Girls tend to become dry at night about a year earlier than boys. What's more, scientists have found a genetic marker highly linked to bedwetting. If one or both parents wet the bed, chances are their children will too. Studies have shown that you can predict when a child will stay dry overnight based on the age that her parents graduated to underwear. Usually it's within a year of when her folks stopped peeing overnight.

Another well-documented pattern: Some kids who have long been dry overnight start wetting the bed after an event that makes them feel anxious or insecure, such as starting a new school, a divorce, the birth of a sibling, the loss of a family member, or moving to a new home. In these cases the bedwetting typically resolves itself within a few months. (Attention-Deficit/Hyperactivity Disorder [ADHD] is also highly linked with bedwetting; see the sidebar, "Attention-Deficit/Hyperactivity Disorder and Bedwetting," on page 105.)

Given these patterns, doctors tend not to be concerned, medically speaking, about young kids who pee in their sleep. They usually tell parents to stick with pull-ups and wait it out. I often give this same advice for children under seven—*if* family members came late to overnight dryness and *if* the child has no history of daytime wetting problems.

BEDWETTING TIDBIT

In one study of four hundred families, the genetic marker associated with bedwetting was found in 90 percent of the families over multiple generations. Other research has shown that children have a 68 percent chance of bedwetting if both parents had the condition and a 44 percent chance if one parent has a bedwetting history.

SOURCES: "ASSIGNMENT OF DOMINANT INHERITED NOCTURNAL ENURESIS (ENURI) TO CHROMOSOME 13Q." EIBERG H, BERENDT I, MOHR J. *NAT GENET.* JUL 1995;10(3):354–56. "PRACTICE PARAMETER FOR THE ASSESSMENT AND TREATMENT OF CHILDREN AND ADOLESCENTS WITH ENURESIS" (PDF). *J . AM. ACAD. CHILD ADOLESC. PSYCHIATRY.* DEC 2004;43(12):1540–50. REVIEW.

But I'm not quick to dismiss bedwetting in a kindergartener who had trouble potty training or a six-year-old who has to sprint to the toilet to pee during the day. And certainly a child age seven or older who has never been dry at night, or who started wetting the bed after a period of dryness, warrants attention. In the vast majority of cases, bedwetting isn't just a nighttime issue; it signals underlying constipation and bladder problems that have developed from bad habits.

Solving these problems almost always cures the bedwetting. Dr. Sean O'Regan's research in the 1980s, spurred by the bedwetting of his five-year-old son (and detailed in Chapter 1), documented this connection convincingly. My own research, including a study coauthored with Evelyn Anthony, M.D., and published in 2012 in the journal *Urology*,[14] supports Dr. O'Regan's findings. Our study reviewed the records of thirty bedwetting patients, average age nine, all of whom were shown by X-ray to be constipated. Aggressive laxative therapy cured all five teenagers in the study within two weeks; laxatives, and in some cases enemas, stopped the bedwetting in 20 of the 25 younger children within three months. Based on Dr. O'Regan's studies and my own, as well as my years of experience, I am convinced that the majority of bedwetting cases are due to a rectum stuffed with poop.

Be aware, however, that in rare cases children who suddenly have started wetting the bed have hidden medical problems, such as an infection or disease, so it's important to rule

---

14 Hodges SI, Anthony EY. Occult Megarectum: A Commonly Unrecognized Cause of Enuresis. *Urology*. Dec 13 2011 [e-pub ahead of print].

out those causes first. For example, a urinary tract infection (UTI) can trigger bedwetting, and in very rare cases, the sudden onset of bedwetting is a symptom of diabetes. These conditions can be detected with a simple urine test, so every child with secondary bedwetting—bedwetting that started after a long period of dryness—should have his urine tested.

Why Kids Wet the Bed

In cases where bedwetting isn't a normal, developmental issue or a sign of infection or disease, it's usually explained in one of three ways: The child is an extraordinarily deep sleeper, she overproduces urine at night, or her bladder can't hold enough urine and has become hyperactive due to holding pee or poop during the day. Of these three causes, I believe that the bladder-capacity/hyperactivity issue is by far the most common, and the other issues may not even exist. Treating a problematic bladder is highly successful, and sometimes, if the problem is entirely related to a poop mass pressing against the child's bladder, the improvement is almost immediate. But if we maximize a child's bladder capacity and the bedwetting persists, I move on to other therapies.

You might wonder: *How can you increase a child's bladder volume? Isn't the size of your bladder predetermined, like the size of your ears?* Not necessarily. If your child's bladder volume has been compromised, either by constipation or the habit of holding pee, there's a lot you can do to expand it. As I explain in Chapter 2, carrying around a belly load full of poop often crowds out the bladder, preventing it from expanding to its full

BEDWETTING TIDBIT

Bedwetting occurs three times more often in boys than in girls.

SOURCE: MILLER K. CONCOMITANT NONPHARMACOLOGIC THERAPY IN THE TREATMENT OF PRIMARY NOCTURNAL ENURESIS. CLIN PEDIATR [PHILA]. 1993;JULY(SPEC. NO.):32–7.

size and causing the nerves that control the bladder to misfire and hiccup. In Chapter 3, I explain how holding pee can shrink bladder capacity by causing the bladder wall to thicken. Many kids have both of these problems, since children who hold poop also tend to hold pee.

If your child is wetting the bed, it is best to assume that his bladder capacity is inadequate (even if he is free of symptoms during the day). And if your child has any history of constipation, daytime accidents, UTIs, or rushing to the bathroom to pee, I would bet my life that an overactive bladder is his number one problem!

In Chapter 3, I detail how to maximize your child's bladder volume, but here's a recap: Make sure your child pees when she wakes up in the morning and roughly every two hours during the day. Two hours before bed she should stop drinking fluids, and she should pee right before bed. You may want to have her pee both before and after the bedtime routine, since most kids are so eager to pop off the potty that they don't empty completely.

Regular, complete emptying—as opposed to holding pee—causes a mild stretching of the bladder, which promotes bladder growth and helps the bladder muscles relax and work as they're supposed to. Our clinic's research has documented that with a program of regular, timed emptying, it takes kids with severely compromised bladder capacity about one year to catch up. This doesn't necessarily mean the child will continue to have wetting problems for a year; if a child's only issue is bedwetting, as opposed to daytime accidents, the wetting may resolve much sooner. But if a child's bladder has become

FROM BEDWETTING TO "BLISS"

One of my patients, Jack Hooten, was in second grade when he started wetting the bed. "It got to the point where we were changing the sheets every night, and he wouldn't spend the night out," recalls his mom, Bailey. "This completely stressed me out and caused tension between me and my husband. I felt like I was not doing a good job as a mom."

Though Bailey didn't know it at the time, Jack's history was classic for a child with bedwetting issues. As a preschooler he'd had a tough time learning to poop on the potty. "He was in a pull-up forever, and we'd constantly have to tell him to go number two," Bailey recalls. "At three, we were giving him candy. At four and five, we upped it to a dollar. By the time he was six, we were promising a trip to Disney World."

Jack often would hold his poop for several days. "And then when he'd finally go," Bailey recalls, "we'd think, 'Great! He got it out.'"

severely thickened, the bladder can take a good while to return to normal.

If constipation has been compromising your child's bladder volume, relieving this poop burden can work miracles. (See the sidebar, "From Bedwetting to 'Bliss,'" on page 96.) Keep in mind that you may have no idea that your child has a pooping problem. Most parents don't. Yet it's almost always an issue in bedwetting. I cannot tell you how many kids I have seen

By age seven, Jack seemed to have turned a corner. He was pooping regularly and was dry at night. But the summer before second grade, he went to sleepaway camp and held his poop the whole week and wet the bed three times. The wetting continued. "We stopped fluids after dinner and were having him empty his bladder before bed," Bailey says. "But none of that helped."

It wasn't until a friend referred her to our clinic that she discovered, via X-ray, that Jack's rectum was stuffed with poop and was practically flattening his bladder. "I was just stunned," Bailey says. "I really thought Jack had some kind of urinary problem that was going to require surgery. I couldn't believe it was just constipation."

Jack did the laxative clean-out described on page 54. "Within two weeks, we were on easy street," says Bailey. "It was like bliss not to have to clean sheets every night and spray down Jack's room with Lysol. It was like a weight had been lifted from all of us. Finally, Jack was feeling really good about himself."

who had been wetting themselves at night for years, suffering unnecessary embarrassment and anxiety, only to become dry within two weeks simply by taking a laxative. Just a tiny fraction of the children or parents even knew that they were constipated or that curing constipation could fix the wetting.

Research confirms that most bedwetting kids, even those with no obvious signs of constipation, will become dry overnight if their bowels are cleared out. Typically, the older the child, the quicker the resolution. In my practice, among teenage bed wetters who are constipated (and almost all teenage bed wetters are), the success rate is close to 100 percent. So if your child wets the bed, go back and read Chapter 2. That may be all you need to get him dry at night. When you treat constipation, do so aggressively. The most common reason for failure is taking a child off laxatives too soon. Don't worry! The laxatives I describe in Chapter 2 for long-term use are extremely safe. Adopting a positive attitude, hokey as this might seem, also has been shown to help stop bedwetting. (See sidebar, "Be Positive, Don't Punish," on page 103 for details.)

BEDWETTING TIDBIT

- *Seventy-five percent of bedwetting cases are "primary," meaning that the child has never been dry overnight.*
- *Twenty-five percent of bedwetting cases are "secondary," meaning the child has been dry for at least six months and then started wetting the bed.*

Calming a Hyperactive Bladder

Maximizing your child's bladder capacity cures bedwetting more often than not, but sometimes, despite the peeing schedule and the intestinal clean out, a child's bladder continues to hiccup overnight because the nerves feeding the bladder are still whacked out. The child's bladder squeezes and empties even before it has a chance to fill completely. In these cases, medication can help the bladder relax.

I discuss medication with parents only if I feel satisfied that all of the child's other issues have been resolved yet she still can't make it two hours without having to pee during the day, or she still rushes to the potty. You'll need to see a pediatric urologist to get a prescription for bladder-relaxing drugs, which are called anticholinergic medications and are known by the brand names such as Ditropan and Detrol. They are most commonly taken in liquid or pill form. I discuss these medicines in Chapter 3.

Measuring your child's bladder capacity also can help determine whether your child is a good candidate for these drugs. I give instructions for this test in Chapter 3 on page 81. If your child's urine volume is less than 70 percent of what is expected for a child of his age, medication may help him stay dry at night.

There are a couple of very important caveats to keep in mind about these medications. Many physicians prescribe them first, without addressing the constipation issues. If you do that, you're headed for failure! These medications can constipate children, so it is critical that the child's bowels are cleaned out before she starts on these drugs. Parents often don't know whether their child is fully unclogged, so read Chapter 2 for a refresher on the signs of and treatments for constipation. The child must stay on a laxative such as MiraLAX while she is taking the medication. Otherwise any benefits from the medications will be negated by the constipation.

Once parents completely address their children's bladder-capacity and overactivity problems, most kids will stay dry at

DON'T TRY THIS: MISGUIDED BEDWETTING "CURES"

Once you've put your child on a peeing schedule, addressed constipation, and given her a pep talk, you've done all you can in terms of behavioral modifications to give her the best chance to be dry. But parents, understandably desperate to cure their child's bedwetting, often resort to other strategies, some of them merely useless, others downright unhealthy. Here's what *not* to do:

• *Don't keep your child in underwear instead of pull-ups so he feels the wetness.* This only serves to punish the child for something that isn't his fault and won't stop him from peeing in his sleep; it'll just make him uncomfortable and cause work for you. For older children, who may be too big for or feel bad about wearing pull-ups, you can find boxers with a concealed pad. Ask your doctor if you can't find them. If your child is using a bedwetting alarm, he can wear pull-ups over the underwear with the sensor attached to the underwear. That way the child feels the wetness but the bed stays dry.

night. If your child still wets the bed, I turn to two other therapies, each addressing a different possible cause of bedwetting.

When Your Child Sleeps through Pee Signals

Pretty much any kid is hard to wake up in the middle of the night, but some kids sleep so deeply that they probably wouldn't flinch if AC/DC were having a concert in their bedroom. One

- *Don't bother with midnight wake ups.* I don't believe it helps to rouse the child from bed during the night and carry or escort her to the bathroom while she's half asleep. It seems that all parents of bed wetters try this approach (many will put the child on the toilet around eleven o'clock or midnight before they themselves go to bed), though I've never seen it work. The problem is that you'll rarely time it correctly. And even if you're able to keep your child dry overnight using this technique, you haven't really solved anything except possibly a laundry problem; you've simply adapted your child's sleeping patterns to her poor bladder capacity. It's a mug's game (one of my favorite British expressions, meaning "a futile endeavor").

- *Don't have your child hold his pee.* There's a myth floating around that holding pee is a good way to stretch a child's bladder, thereby allowing his bladder to hold more urine at night. In truth, holding pee is unhealthy for a child's bladder, straining and thickening the bladder wall and actually shrinking bladder capacity. Peeing on a schedule, before the child even gets the signal to go, is what promotes bladder growth, as I explain in Chapter 3.

theory of bedwetting is that some of these kids sleep through signals that their bladders are full and, instead of waking up and walking to the bathroom, wet the bed. But this theory is not well supported by research. I think this notion comes from parents who have trouble waking up their kids who wet the bed but who don't have any experience trying to wake up their other children. Their siblings who don't wet the bed may very well sleep just as deeply.

Nonetheless, bedwetting alarms can work well by training your child to wake up before he wets the bed. If your child is a deep sleeper, he may be a good candidate for this therapy. Just keep in mind that the alarm is not a substitute for addressing the constipation and bladder-capacity issues that are likely preventing your child from being able to last all night without having to pee. The alarm is a tool to use in addition to the strategies discussed in this chapter.

A bedwetting alarm rings after the child has wet herself. Though it seems counterintuitive to wake the child *after* she pees, eventually this process teaches her to wake up when she needs to go. A bedwetting alarm can be bought without a prescription and, unlike medication, has no risks or side effects— well, other than parental grouchiness from having your sleep interrupted every night for weeks.

A bedwetting alarm includes a urine-sensor patch that can either be placed in the child's underwear or on the sheet underneath him. The sensor is attached to an alarm that clips to his shirt and rings when the sensor gets wet. (You can buy fancy wireless alarms with remote sensors for parents, but the

BE POSITIVE, DON'T PUNISH

I believe that most cases of bedwetting are related to constipation and bladder overactivity, but no doubt there's also a psychological component to bedwetting. I know kids who are dry every time they sleep at Grandma and Grandpa's house yet wet at home, and kids who went from dry overnight to drenched once school started. Clearly, major life changes can trigger bedwetting.

Maintaining a positive attitude can help; punishing or shaming your child for wetting the bed is absolutely harmful. Most bed wetters feel bad enough about their problem, so rather than make your child feel embarrassed or ashamed, encourage him and praise him on dry mornings.

Don't assume that your child's bedwetting indicates that she has psychological or behavioral problems. Multiple studies have found kids who frequently wet the bed are no more likely than other kids to be anxious or depressed. (However, ADHD kids do have higher bedwetting rates; see the sidebar "Attention-Deficit/Hyperactivity Disorder and Bedwetting," page 105.) Often it's the bedwetting that leads to anxiety, not the other way around. After successful treatment for the bedwetting, these kids are much happier and more relaxed.

extra expense isn't necessary; unless you and your child live on opposite sides of a mansion, you'll hear the alarm.) Often, the child does not wake up when the alarm sounds, which means Mom and Dad have to wake him up and turn off the alarm, take the child to the bathroom and have him try to pee, help him change clothes, place the alarm back on, and go back to bed. Yes, I know what you're thinking: *That's too exhausting! I have a job! I have other kids!* But it works. When the alarm is used properly, more than 80 percent of kids get dry within three months.

Alarm therapy has a bad reputation because many people have tried it without success. But that's usually because parents give up when the alarm doesn't wake the child. (Some parents may abandon ship because the wetting doesn't stop, not realizing that it's constipation, rather than deep sleeping, that is causing the wetting and even waking up won't stop an overactive bladder.) I'm not minimizing how miserable it can be to try to wake a child who seems to be sleeping in a near-comatose state. It can seem as futile as trying to wake a sofa. But if you are going to try the alarm, it's important to decide as a family that you will give it your best effort. Be patient. It often takes at least two weeks to see any improvement and up to three months for total success. While you are using this strategy, remind your child that it's okay to use the toilet during the night. Put nightlights in key places so your child can easily find her way to the bathroom.

The Last Resort
A theory popular among some physicians holds that in some kids bedwetting is linked to overproducing urine at night, possibly due to a hormonal imbalance. The theory holds that at night these children don't produce enough antidiuretic

ATTENTION-DEFICIT/HYPERACTIVITY DISORDER AND BEDWETTING

Kids with Attention-Deficit/Hyperactivity Disorder (ADHD) are two to six times more likely to wet the bed than kids without ADHD, just as they're more likely to have accidents and be constipated. ADHD kids are also harder to treat for bedwetting. In a Mayo Clinic study, for example, 68 percent of children with ADHD overcame bedwetting with therapies such as those described in this chapter, compared to 91 percent of kids without ADHD. The same study found that some 48 percent of the kids had trouble sticking with the treatment plan, compared to just 14 percent of the non-ADHD kids. Among kids in the study who used the bedwetting alarm, 66 percent of children without ADHD had long-term success, compared to 19 percent of the ADHD kids.

None of this is surprising: Kids who have trouble focusing tend to spend less time on the potty, so often they don't fully empty their bladder and bowels. If your child already is being treated for ADHD, it's fine to go ahead with the treatments described in this chapter. Just make sure the ADHD is being addressed and be patient. It may take your child longer to resolve her bedwetting problem.

hormone (ADH), a hormone that limits urine production. The data behind this theory are iffy, and I am skeptical of this explanation, because virtually all bedwetting can be cured by fixing constipation and bladder overactivity and, if necessary, using a bedwetting alarm. However, I'm not completely discounting the possibility that some kids do produce excess urine at night, and that's why they wet the bed. If these kids also are deep sleepers and no other treatment seems to work, it may be worth considering a drug called desmopressin, sold as DDVAP (which replaces the lacking ADH). This medicine affects the hormones that control urine production, tricking the kidneys into making less urine at night. DDVAP is completely different from bladder-relaxing medicines, like Detrol or Ditropan, which act on the bladder muscle itself.

I consider desmopressin purely a stopgap measure, a last resort worth trying only in limited circumstances, like getting a stressed-out child through a week at sleepaway camp. The drug is very effective but only in the short-term. When kids stop taking the medication, they usually start wetting the bed again, so the drug doesn't really fix the problem but rather covers it up. Children who have been treated with desmopressin should not stop taking the drug cold turkey; they should be weaned slowly.

Desmopressin works quickly (a two-week trial can determine the appropriate dose), and it's generally safe, although in rare cases it can interfere with electrolyte levels. In fact, some research found that elderly patients taking this drug experience dangerous drops in their sodium levels. So I would not want a child on desmopressin for more than six months. The idea of altering the hormones that control urine output in children doesn't sit well with me. We urologists have a saying: A dumb kidney is smarter than a smart doctor. In other words,

BEDWETTING BY THE NUMBERS

50: Percent of three-year-olds who wet overnight.

20: Percent of five-year-olds who wet overnight.

7: Percent of eight-year-olds who wet overnight.

5: Percent of ten-year-olds who wet overnight.

SOURCE: BENNETT H.J. *WAKING UP DRY: A GUIDE TO HELP CHILDREN OVERCOME BEDWETTING.* ELK GROVE VILLAGE, IL: AMERICAN ACADEMY OF PEDIATRICS.

if you're producing a lot of urine at night and are otherwise healthy, there is probably a darned good reason your body is making that pee. We all need to get rid of fluid to maintain our body's fluid and electrolyte balance, so why mess with that?

Prescribing a drug is easy for a doctor and often reassures exhausted, distressed parents that something is being done. But in almost all cases of bedwetting, I feel a more thorough evaluation of the causes of overnight peeing is warranted.

Keep It Simple

If you follow the instructions in this chapter, you're almost certain to have success treating your child's bedwetting. A tiny fraction of children may have extremely severe bladder overactivity requiring more extensive interventions; a pediatric urologist can explain these if they pertain to your child. But almost all kids can enjoy dry, stress-free nights with simple measures.

CHAPTER 5

Urinary Tract Infections: Myths, Truths, and Cures

OK, moms and dads, it's pop quiz time! The best way to prevent urinary tract infections (UTIs) in a young girl is to make sure she:

A. Always wipes from front to back.

B. Takes showers instead of baths.

C. Avoids drinking soda.

D. A and B.

E. None of the above.

I won't keep you in suspense. The answer is E. But if you didn't guess correctly, don't sweat it. When it comes to UTIs, there's no shortage of mythology floating around the Internet, moms' clubs, even pediatricians' offices. Let me add one more misconception: Little girls don't get UTIs. In fact, 5 to 7 percent of girls age three to ten have had a UTI, and the recurrence rate is high. Some of my patients have been referred to me after getting infection after infection, sometimes ten or twelve in a year! A new UTI develops just as soon as the last one has cleared up.

In this chapter I explain the real reasons UTIs are so common in young girls—reasons that have plenty to do with constipation and holding pee and nothing to do with wiping, baths, or drinking soda. I also explain why, despite treatment with antibiotics, UTIs come back so often and what you can do to keep your daughter infection free.

What Exactly Is a UTI?

Here's a fact that may surprise you: Urine is sterile. You could literally drink it and be fine (although I don't recommend it as a beverage). Urine is mostly water, with a small percentage of harmless waste products. My point is: Urine is not like poop; it should be bacteria free. But sometimes certain types of bacteria gain access to the bladder and grow in the urine. The upshot: a bladder infection, also known as a urinary tract infection.

To get a UTI, you need a source of bacteria, a pathway for this bacteria to enter the bladder, and a bladder full of urine for the bacteria to grow in. UTI-causing bacteria can sometimes be found on the skin of the perineum, around your bottom, but all of these bacteria come from the stool itself. (The bacteria that normally live on your skin, such as on your hands, do not cause UTIs.) Sometimes bacteria from poop enter the urinary tract by crawling up the skin between the anus and urethra into the bladder. There they set up shop and multiply, causing pain and irritation.

You can prevent these infections by getting rid of the source of bacteria, making the path to the bladder inhospitable, or keeping the bladder empty. As I explain in this chapter, young girls typically do none of these things, which is why they are perfect candidates for UTIs.

Young boys have the same unhealthy potty habits as girls, but they almost never get UTIs because of their anatomy. In a girl, bacteria have a much shorter distance to travel from the anus to the bladder because her urethra is shorter. UTIs in boys are rare enough that a doctor needs to evaluate the child for a congenital anomaly of the urinary tract that is preventing him from fully emptying his pee.

Diagnosing a UTI

In young girls the symptoms of a UTI are peeing too often, painful peeing, and the sudden onset of daytime accidents or bedwetting. Some parents swear they can smell a UTI, that the child's urine has a particular foul odor, but research has shown that this isn't the case (moms who claimed to be able to smell infected urine were as wrong as they were right). In rare cases the child also has a fever above 101.5°F accompanied by nausea, vomiting, and belly or side/kidney pain. These are signs that the infection has traveled from the bladder to the kidneys, a more severe situation that may signal the type of anatomical problem I mention in the sidebar, "The Exceptions: UTIs Not Caused by Potty Problems," on page 111.

We diagnose a UTI by collecting a urine sample in the office and checking it with a dipstick, a strip of paper that can

THE EXCEPTIONS:
UTIS NOT CAUSED BY POTTY PROBLEMS

Not every UTI is caused by unhealthy potty habits. Some girls get UTIs because their urinary tracts are obstructed, either by stones or by some congenital blockage, and the urine just sits there. Stones develop when the salt concentration in urine gets too high, and the salts crystallize, either because the child doesn't drink enough or because she's genetically predisposed. A blockage may need to be fixed by removing the stone or by excising the narrow area in the ureter obstructing the urinary tract, although some congenital obstructions resolve on their own.

Other girls are simply more prone to UTIs because they have bladders that are extra "sticky"; in other words, bacteria tend to stick to the bladder wall. For these girls the only way to prevent UTIs is to follow the advice discussed in this chapter: Pee more often, poop more often, and keep the vagina clean and dry.

Then there are the kids who develop UTIs, along with a fever over 101.5°F (known as pyelonephritis, a kidney infection), due to urinary reflex. In other words, when the child pees, some of the urine flows up from the bladder to the kidneys instead of out the urethra. Urinary reflux is caused by a faulty valve at the junction of the ureters and the bladder. Though this is a congenital problem that many children outgrow, it's much less likely to resolve without surgery if a child is holding poop and/or pee. Urinary reflux is the condition that I diagnosed in Ella, the patient I describe in Chapter 1 who changed the course of my career.

indicate the presence of blood or other markers of infection. If the dipstick looks suspicious, we examine a sample under a microscope. If we determine the child has a simple UTI, one that is not accompanied by a fever, we treat it with three days of antibiotics. A UTI with a fever needs seven to ten days of antibiotics. In severe cases the child might need to be hospitalized for IV antibiotics.

But antibiotics aren't the end of the story—not by a long shot. I frequently see patients who have been treated by a pediatrician with medication only to return a month later with another infection. That's because antibiotics do nothing to attack the root of the problem.

The Real Reasons Kids Get UTIs

I treat UTIs for a living. I see all types, thousands each year. Do you know how often I see a UTI in a child who isn't toilet trained? Never. Do you know how many UTIs I see in girls who recently have toilet trained or are in the process of training? A ton.

There's no doubt the peeing and pooping habits of kids in diapers are much healthier than those of toilet-trained children. That's one reason I favor postponing potty training until a child is at least three years old; the longer you put off this transition for the child, the less time she has to develop bad habits. But all kids need to be potty trained, of course, so at some point even those trained on a later schedule are susceptible to the unhealthy behaviors that increase the risk for developing UTIs. I'm talking about three habits in particular: holding pee, holding poop, and peeing with their legs closed.

Why would holding pee cause a UTI? This is easy to explain when you look at a picture of the urinary tract (see Figure 5-1). The bladder almost always has some pee in it, except right after it's emptied. You manage to stay dry because the bladder neck, the part of the bladder that connects to the urethra, automatically stays closed when you aren't peeing. The rest of the urethra is an open tube and always houses bacteria, some of which may have come from the poop. These bacteria are always trying to climb up into the bladder, looking for unexplored country. Women don't get UTIs often because they pee regularly and drink plenty; every time they pee, they wash the bacteria out of the urethra. The salmon are trying to

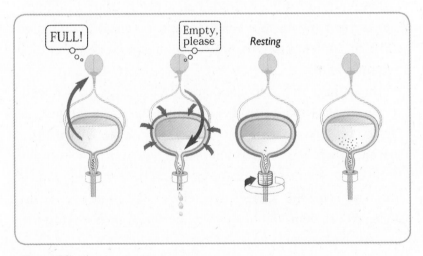

Figure 5-1
Holding urine can lead to urinary tract infections by allowing bacteria in the urethra to gain access to the bladder.

swim upstream, so to speak, and the more you pee, the harder you make it for them.

The less often you pee, the more opportunity for the bacteria to creep up to the bladder. Here's where things go awry for young girls. Not only do they fail to pee regularly, but they also actively suppress the urge to pee. The holding habit ratchets up the risk of infection. Let's say you need to pee really badly. What you are feeling is the bladder actively contracting because it's reached a certain volume level. As that happens, the bladder neck automatically opens because it thinks you are going to pee. But suppose you're nowhere near a toilet at that moment you feel the urge. The only way to stay dry at that point is to squeeze your urethral sphincter (a different muscle from the anal sphincter, the one you squeeze to hold in poop, though they often act in concert). This signals the spinal cord to make the bladder stop contracting, as I explain in detail in Chapter 3. The urge goes away, but the pee stays put.

Sometimes the child augments this by sitting on her heels or dancing around. (Yes, this actually helps keep the pee in; try it!) So look at what happens: The urine enters into the urethra, where the bacteria are hanging out, but it doesn't get flushed out. Instead it picks up bacteria. Then the urge to pee goes away and the bladder neck closes. The bacteria pick up an expressway into the bladder, riding the urine back into the bladder. Next stop: UTI.

The fact that babies never get UTIs suggests that pee holding is the single most common cause of these infections in girls. Constipation and skin irritation surely can cause UTIs, but I believe urine holding plays a bigger role because we don't see a spike in the number of infections until kids toilet train, even though children often experience constipation or skin irritation before learning to use the potty. The solution is simple: Have the child pee more often. As I mention in Chapter 3 (now is a good time to go back and read it!), the trick is to place the child on a schedule so that she pees about every two hours. Instruct your daughter to pee rather than ask whether she needs to go, since she'll always say no. Make sure she takes her time and empties her bladder fully. If you see your child doing the potty dance, squatting, or curtseying to hold her pee, you know that she's in the habit of holding. It makes me nuts when people or ads poke fun at the potty dance. This is serious, folks!

The Poop-UTI Connection

Getting your child to pee more often prevents the offending bacteria from entering the bladder, but how do you stop the bacteria from taking hold to begin with—how do you cut off the supply line, so to speak? As I mentioned earlier, all bacteria that cause UTIs originate from poop, traveling to the bladder via the skin. Since everyone poops, you can't very well cut off access to this bacteria, right? Wrong!

Let's go back to our old friend constipation. Kids who are constipated carry around a hefty load of poop, primarily in the rectum. Well, guess what is in a ton of poop? A gazillion bazillion bacteria (to be precise)—about a gazillion times more than when the rectum has been emptied of poop. What's more, studies have shown that when you have a pile of poop sitting in the rectum, bacteria mutate and you end up with more of the bacteria that are able to cause UTIs and fewer of the bacteria that can't. And you know what is a couple of inches from the rectum? Yep, the bladder. The offending bacteria crawl through the perineal skin and into the vagina and the area around the urethra. The way to make it hard for the offending bacteria to journey to the bladder is to fully treat constipation. I trust you are picking up a pattern here!

For girls who are constipated, clearing out a mass of poop in the rectum is almost a surefire way to put an end to UTIs, as Dr. O'Regan showed back in the 1980s and a number of studies have shown since. As you might recall from Chapter 1, Dr. O'Regan followed forty-seven girls who had recurrent UTIs and were severely constipated. After three months on the doctor's favorite enema regimen, forty-four of the girls stopped getting infections.

Staying Clean, Dry, and Infection-Free

I've told you how peeing more and pooping more can prevent UTIs. Now I'll explain how keeping the vagina clean and dry helps the situation.

Here's a little-known factoid: Menopausal women have a higher rate of UTIs than women who are actively menstruating. This is related to the pH of the vagina. When women are actively producing estrogen, the vagina is acidic, and it's harder for UTI-causing bacteria to live there. When women

SOOTHING BATHS FOR GIRLS

If your daughter is experiencing vaginal irritation, old-fashioned home remedies such as oatmeal, vinegar, and baking soda baths can offer relief, though Aveeno baths may be easier because you don't have to grind up the oatmeal or use soap in addition. If you want to use soap, Cetaphil Restoraderm cleanser is an excellent choice to avoid irritation. Try any of these baths daily until the redness disappears. Have your daughter open and close her legs to swirl around the water and get it flowing deeper into her vagina.

- *Oatmeal bath.* Any type of plain oatmeal is fine; avoid flavored varieties. Grind up the oats as finely as possible in a blender, food processor, or coffee grinder. How fine is fine enough? Add a spoonful of the powder to a glass of water and stir; if the liquid is milky and little settles on the bottom, you're good to go. While the tub is filling, add one cup of oatmeal powder to the bath and swirl it around with your arm.
- *Vinegar bath.* Because vinegar is an acid, you might think it would be harsh on irritated skin, but in fact it's gentle, counteracting the basic nature of urine. Fill the tub, measure one cup of vinegar, and splash it in the bath.
- *Baking soda bath.* Add about four tablespoons of baking soda to a filled tub. Baking soda acts a lot like oatmeal, soothing and healing red, irritated skin.

are not producing estrogen, which is what happens after menopause, the pH of the vagina is neutral and bacteria grow like crazy.

As it turns out, the pH of a vagina before puberty also is neutral. This is one reason why young girls are so susceptible to UTIs. Of course you can't go around putting girls on estrogen, which is a common treatment for menopausal women with recurrent UTIs. So how can you compensate for the pH predicament and lower a girl's chances of getting a UTI?

You keep the skin between the anus and vagina clean and dry. At our clinic we noticed that all the girls we were seeing for recurrent UTIs had red, irritated skin along their labia majora. Most of these girls had been treated for yeast by their pediatricians, even though the redness is typically not caused by yeast. What does cause redness is peeing with the legs together, which is what girls often do. (This is called vaginal voiding, and I explain it in Chapter 3.) The skin between the labia stays wet from the urine, and some of the pee enters the vagina and drips out later, making the vagina even damper, as urine is a skin irritant. This redness and irritation is called vulvitis. Pediatricians often confuse this with yeast and treat it with an antifungal, which doesn't help.

In a study, our clinic evaluated the skin of fifty girls with vulvitis and fifty girls without irritation. In the children without skin irritation we tended to find typical, noninfectious skin and vaginal bugs. But in the girls with irritated skin, we almost always found E. coli or Enterococcus, the two most common UTI-causing bacteria. This is related to the pH issue. The pH of skin is supposed to be acidic, but when the skin is irritated, it loses its protective acid mantle and becomes neutral, providing a pleasant pathway for bacteria from the rectum to the urethra. We call this the pH bridge.

It's easy to tear down this pH bridge. First of all, little girls should always pee with their legs spread (picture sitting on the toilet backward), so the area doesn't stay so wet. Plus they must wipe well on the inside, keeping all skin that is touching other skin clean and dry. It's also helpful to use diaper cream overnight, either petroleum jelly or zinc oxide–based agents, or the skin may become irritated. Some colleagues and I have created *pottyRx Healthy Wipes*, which contain an astringent that restores skin pH to counteract the effects of the urine and are available at pottyrx.com.

Dispelling Common Myths About UTIs

I recently had a mom tell me she had tried every remedy her pediatrician had recommended to prevent her daughter's recurrent UTIs: She made certain her daughter wiped from front to back, she stopped giving her baths, and she even had the girl stop drinking anything red. *Stop drinking anything red?!* That was a new one to me. I don't know where these myths come from, but it's not from science, I assure you. Here I review the most common misconceptions about urinary tract infections.

Wiping from Front to Back

Virtually every parent of a UTI patient has told me she makes sure her daughter wipes from front to back, so she can't figure out why the child keeps getting infections. Most moms are shocked by my response: There is absolutely no evidence that wiping from front to back helps prevent UTIs. I don't go around promoting back-to-front wiping, but I actually feel confident that it wouldn't do any harm.

Let me put it this way: Remember when your daughter was a baby, and she'd poop in her diaper and the poop would squish all over her entire genital area? Did she ever get an infection? Nope. It's not the direction of wiping that matters. The important thing is keeping the area clean and dry, especially the area between the labia where skin is touching. Think of it like this: If you put a saltwater fish in a fresh-water tank, the fish would die. Sure, it's in water, but not the right type of environment for it to live. Much the same way, you can put E. coli on healthy skin and it won't live because the pH kills it; only when the pH is accommodating can the bacteria live.

Taking a Bath

Parents constantly tell me that they have their three-year-olds taking showers because they are afraid baths will cause a UTI. I'm not sure where this idea originated, but avoiding baths is misguided for several reasons. First, most little girls have pee up in their vagina all day long, so sitting in a tub of water can only help clean that out. Second, while it's true that garden-variety lye-based soaps, like Ivory, can irritate the labial skin, cause vulvitis, and possibly increase UTI risk, the solution is not to avoid baths. The answer is to avoid irritating soaps, which strip off the protective coating of the skin. (Choose soaps that you would use on your face; these are gentler on the skin and usually pH balanced, a good one is Cetaphil Restoraderm.) I also recommend that little girls soak in Aveeno. Your daughter gets plenty clean, and the Aveeno, made from very finely ground oatmeal, soothes the skin, and actually makes things better. You can get a similar effect from homemade baths using ground-up supermarket oatmeal, baking soda, or vinegar (see the sidebar, "Soothing Baths for Girls," on page 117).

Drinking Soda

While we are at it, let's attack one of the strangest yet most pervasive UTI myths: Soda causes infection. I hear this all the time from patients. I don't care what you drink; it all comes out as pee. Drinking soda is a bad idea because it's a source of empty calories and lousy for teeth, but there's absolutely no connection between soda and UTIs. I'm guessing people make this mistaken connection because caffeine, common in sodas, can irritate the bladder, making it contract more. But soda certainly doesn't cause UTIs.

While we're on the subject of beverages, know that drinking cranberry juice is not an effective treatment for UTIs. In high doses cranberry juice may help prevent infections, ostensibly by making it harder for bacteria to stick to the bladder. However, that theory has never held up in good studies, and there's definitely no connection between cranberry juice and UTI treatment.

So that about covers it. If your daughter pees on time and poops on time and her bottom stays clean, dry, and free of irritation, she can't get a UTI. It is against the laws of nature.

CHAPTER 6

Other Potty Problems: Frequent Peeing, Painful Peeing, and Blood in the Urine

Accidents and bedwetting are the urinary problems that parents worry about most, but many kids who are able to stay dry 24/7 have other pee issues. Some of these kids pee too often. Some feel pain when they pee—pain that is unrelated to urinary tract infections (UTIs). Other kids have small amounts of blood in their urine. If you've read the other chapters in this book, you will not be shocked to learn that these three problems typically have the same root cause: constipation.

In this chapter I explain how carrying around a belly load of poop triggers these particular peeing problems and how you can put a stop to them.

Peeing Too Often

Too-frequent peeing, a condition known as urinary frequency, is defined as peeing more often than eight times a day. But don't bother counting. With this condition you know it when you see it. These kids pee *all the time*, as often as every few minutes. Their incessant trips to the toilet disrupt lives (theirs and yours), get these kids in trouble at school, and are really annoying when you are trying to drive farther than the end of your block.

Urinary frequency is, for reasons unknown, far more common in boys than in girls. It typically shows up in four-year-olds, probably because it takes a year or two after potty training for constipation problems to reach a critical point. But kids of all ages can develop this problem. Parents understandably become alarmed when their preschooler starts peeing more often than a pregnant woman. Since the child actually produces pee each time he visits the toilet, Mom and Dad assume he's generating gallons of urine and jump to the conclusion that he has diabetes. Indeed excessive urinating is a symptom of diabetes, but as I mention in Chapter 3, I've examined hundreds of kids with urinary frequency whose parents feared diabetes, and exactly zero were diabetic.

So if your child has urinary frequency, don't panic! To be on the safe side, have a simple urine test performed on your child; this can rule out infection or the rare case of diabetes. But I can already tell you the test is going to be normal. The real culprit is constipation. Your kid is peeing too often because his rectum is stuffed with poop.

This is not a widely recognized explanation because so little research has been conducted on kids with frequency problems. Back in the 1980s, researchers at Ohio State University conducted one of the few studies ever published on this topic.[15] The researchers reviewed records in forty-three

---

15   Koff SA, Byard MA. The daytime urinary frequency syndrome of childhood. *J Urol.* Nov 1988;140(5 Pt 2):1280–81.

fully toilet-trained children with this problem, testing the kids' urine, performing ultrasounds on their kidneys, and asking their parents if the children were pooping normally. The researchers detected no problems and concluded that urinary-frequency problems in childhood come out of the blue, may have behavioral causes, and typically disappear on their own within a few months.

For two decades that's all doctors had to go on. But after evaluating thousands of children with bladder problems, my colleagues and I began to suspect that constipation plays a role in urinary frequency, the way it clearly does in all the other bladder-related problems we've studied. So we did our own investigation. Like the Ohio State researchers, we followed forty-three children with this condition, ages three to eight. But we went further. Instead of asking parents whether their children had pooping problems, we asked them to rate their children's poops using the Bristol Stool Scale (see Figure 2-1, page 37) and X-rayed their abdomens. We found that 80 percent of these kids were carrying a significant poop burden and that unclogging their rectums reduced their constant trips to the toilet rather dramatically. Within two weeks they were peeing normally.

As I detail in Chapter 2, a clog in the rectum can set off a chain reaction. The pelvic nerves, the very nerves that control the bladder, go haywire, sending faulty—and terribly frequent—signals to the bladder that it's time to pee. What's more, the child experiences a simple mass effect: The mondo load of poop crowds out the bladder so it can't hold enough urine to last longer than a few minutes between voids. In extreme cases the poop mass encroaches on the bladder so much that it blocks the bladder outlet, and the child is unable to fully empty. Incomplete emptying, in turn, causes frequent peeing. To get a better picture of what's happening, imagine a large glass that is being continually filled with water. If you empty that glass completely, it will take longer to refill than if you empty it only a tiny bit. The same applies to bladders that don't empty well: They get refilled rapidly after the child pees, and the child is constantly heading to the toilet.

In all these scenarios the child is actually peeing, so parents understandably get the impression that their child is turning out rivers of urine. In actuality these kids are just peeing smaller amounts more frequently. One mom told me that after she'd put her three-and-a-half-year-old son to bed, he would come to pee five or six times—every night! He was a defiant kid, and she thought he was just coming out to push his parents' buttons and get a reaction. He succeeded there! The mom told me, "How can a kid possibly produce that much urine?" As it turned out the child was seriously constipated. Once a laxative regimen cleared him out, he stopped making multiple trips to the bathroom after bedtime.

Frequency problems are almost always caused by constipation, but there's actually one condition, in addition to diabetes, that does cause kids to overproduce urine and is not related to a poop mass. It's called psychogenic polydipsia, a compulsion to drink large amounts of water. Kids who have this condition drink as if they've been lost in the desert for weeks, even though their bodies are not low on fluid. This urge to imbibe excessively is poorly understood—one theory is that these kids drink for emotional reasons—but in any case, parents usually pick up on the constant drinking as well as the constant peeing, so the incessant trips to the toilet are no mystery. If you drink two liters, you'll pee two liters. If your child seems to be drinking far more than normal, measure his intake as best you can and bring this information to your doctor. Just know that psychogenic polydipsia is unbelievably rare; in fact, I haven't come across a single case.

So if your child is peeing so often that it's disrupting her life, or yours, I recommend rereading Chapter 2. The remedies described there, primarily a daily dose of MiraLAX or a generic equivalent, should fix your child's frequency problem within a few weeks. A child whose only urinary issue is frequency is more likely to be cured quickly than a kid who also has accidents and/or wets the bed.

One peculiar note: I've heard pediatricians blame urinary frequency in boys on an extrasmall pee hole, known as meatal stenosis. The theory goes that the hole is so tiny that only a small portion of the pee held in the bladder can make its way out. In reality, every circumcised boy has some degree of meatal stenosis, because the opening of the urethra scars a bit when it's exposed to the outside world following circumcision. But in no way does the size of a boy's pee hole prevent him from fully emptying his pee. On occasion this scarring causes a child's pee stream to deflect upward and makes a mess of the bathroom, in which case it needs to be fixed—give me a call.

Painful Peeing

Painful peeing, known as dysuria, is a classic sign of a urinary tract infection (UTI). If your daughter winces when she pees or is afraid to pee because it hurts, absolutely get her urine tested for infection. But what if her pee is normal? You can assume she's constipated, and the poop clog is causing the discomfort.

It's unclear how exactly this poop mass causes painful urination, but in my clinic we've seen this association many times, and intuitively it makes sense. It can't feel great to pee when you have a large, hard mass pressing on your bladder neck and the nerves of the pelvic wall. The most convincing part of this theory is that when we clear the poop out of these kids (poop that's evident in X-rays), the pain always disappears. At my clinic we've X-rayed countless girls and boys whose only symptom is painful peeing or who complain of painful peeing accompanied by intermittent belly pain. Invariably, unclogging their intestines using the methods described in Chapter 2 does the trick.

Painful Peeing in Girls: An Exception

There's one type of painful peeing that's unrelated either to constipation or infection. It happens only in girls, and it's caused by vulvitis, or inflammation of the skin around the vagina. As I explain in Chapter 3, when little girls pee, they often don't wipe well, or they pee with their legs together, so that a lot of the urine goes up in the vagina, only to drip out later. Either way the end result is the same: Pee wets the skin around the vagina, causing skin irritation and a rash. This rash, which also can be caused by skin irritants such as bubble bath, makes girls feel a burning sensation when they pee.

An oatmeal bath is a great alternative to soap, and oatmeal, vinegar, or baking soda baths can often provide immediate relief. See Chapter 5 for instructions. To prevent future rashes, have your daughter pee with her legs apart, either by pulling her pants all the way down, or off, or by having her sit on the toilet backward. Make sure she wipes well, especially on the inside. Slathering diaper creams on the skin of this area, especially at night, can provide relief, as can pottyRx Healthy Wipes (available at pottyrx.com).

Blood in the Urine

Blood in the urine, known as hematuria, always warrants a visit to a doctor and comes in several forms. In some cases blood is visible in the entire stream of pee. In others, you can't see the blood without a microscope; these cases are usually picked up on routine urine tests during annual checkups with the pediatrician. Both of these forms of hematuria rarely are related to peeing and pooping problems and warrant referral to a kidney doctor, also known as a nephrologist. When associated with swollen joints and high blood pressure, blood in the urine can be a sign of kidney disease. Kidney disease is very rare in children, much more rare than hematuria, but it's a serious condition and important to detect and treat promptly, so that's why we look.

But there's one form of hematuria, present only in boys, that is related to constipation and/or holding pee. In these cases the blood is visible only at the end of the stream. This means the blood originated at the bladder neck, where the bladder meets the urethra. In preadolescent boys this area often bleeds as a result of high pressure, usually due to holding pee too long or a large poop mass. If you notice blood at the end of your child's pee stream, have him evaluated by a physician, but also know that having him pee on a schedule and treating him for constipation will usually clear up the problem.

Constipation: The Root of All Problems?

Now I know what you're thinking: *This guy blames every childhood problem on constipation.* Not true! I am willing to concede that separation anxiety, video game addiction, and sibling rivalry are in no way caused by constipation. I'll give you that. But the reality is almost all toileting difficulties are indeed related to stopped-up intestines, and these problems almost always resolve when the constipation clears up. If you're skeptical, have your pediatrician X-ray your child's belly. Make sure she actually looks at the X-ray instead of just reading the report. Most radiologists, unless specifically asked, don't comment on how much poop they see on an X-ray, so many films that are full of poop may be read as normal.

CHAPTER 7

Scary Bathrooms, Foolish Rules, and Other Ways School Can Make a Healthy Kid Sick

When Cici Carter, a sixteen-year-old from Greenville, North Carolina, came to my clinic with her mom, she'd had a urinary tract infection (UTI) every month of the school year. I figured out why after asking exactly one question: Do you go to the bathroom at school?

Cici looked at me sideways, as if I'd asked, "Do you enjoy lap swimming in raw sewage?"

She said no, of course she didn't use the school restrooms, adding, "I don't know many people who do."

The only remarkable thing about Cici's case was that she'd made it to high school without developing a UTI. Most kids who hold their pee or poop all day—yes, *all* day, from 7:30 a.m. to 4:00 p.m.—end up with urinary problems at a far younger age. (I explain the connection between holding pee or poop and UTIs in Chapter 5.) Everything else Cici told me I had heard before, thousands of times: The stalls were littered with wadded up toilet paper. The sinks were clogged with hair, the walls marred by graffiti. The toilet water was yellow—or brown. Sometimes the bathrooms had soap but no paper towels, other times paper towels but no soap. The place reeked.

"There were times after lunch when I felt completely bloated, and I knew I had to go to the bathroom," Cici told me. "But I wasn't about to use it. No way." Even if Cici had wanted to brave the restroom, at any time other than lunch or the short breaks between classes, she knew her teachers would say, "Oh, you'll be all right. Just wait until the bell." That was the response she'd heard when other kids asked.

If your child hasn't entered the public school system, you may find Cici's story to be an exaggeration or an exception. Just wait! According to various surveys, between 20 and 40 percent of middle-school and high-school students avoid using school bathrooms because they consider them dirty or unsafe. As for younger children, they face their own toileting-related challenges at school. What happened to Zoe Rosso and her family may have been unusual in some respects—three-year-olds don't often get suspended from school for potty infractions—but the medical problems she experienced are commonly triggered or exacerbated by school toilet-training policies. Remember back in the 1980s when so little was understood about AIDS that Ryan White, the seventh grader who'd contracted HIV through a blood transfusion, was banned from his school? Well, when it comes to children's toileting issues, schools today, from preschool through high school, are basically at that same level of awareness.

I know public schools are besieged. Given the pressure to boost test scores in the face of dwindling funding, discipline problems, and teacher layoffs, the condition of the bathroom soap dispensers doesn't rate high on any school's list of priorities. But it should. The difference between a clean, safe bathroom and one that is smelly and scary may be the difference between a child staying healthy and the same child developing bladder problems that plague him for a lifetime. Plus, I'm guessing that students who aren't doubled over in pain from holding their pee for six hours learn more in class than their peers who regularly relieve themselves.

In this chapter I explain how, at all school levels, policies, bathroom conditions, and a lack of awareness among administrators, teachers, and school nurses are contributing to our potty-problem epidemic. What can a parent really do about these problems? Glad you asked. I have plenty of ideas. But since I spend my days ultrasounding bladders and examining urine-flow patterns, I turned for additional suggestions to the country's foremost advocate for school bathroom cleanliness and safety, Georgia educator Tom Keating, Ph.D. Dr. Keating, also known as "Bathroom Man" and "that toilet guy," is founder of Project CLEAN (Citizens, Learners, and Educators Against Neglect), a remarkable initiative to make school restrooms a place where kids actually will go to pee. Though it's a task that redefines "uphill battle," Dr. Keating is not deterred and says you should not be either. "Improving school bathrooms is not about money," he told me. "It's about changing the attitudes and behavior of students and finding more parents and administrators who will address the issues. We need to raise hell. These kids are starved for our help."

The Problem with Preschools

As I mention in other chapters, I don't think children under age three should be in charge of their own toileting habits any more than they should be in charge of their college funds. Young kids simply don't have the good judgment to pee or poop in a timely manner. Symptoms may not surface for two or three years, but the holding behavior so common among potty-trained two-year-olds often catches up with these kids. That's when they show up at my clinic, with the sudden onset of accidents, UTIs, urinary frequency, or numerous other problems.

In the scientific literature and articles online, you can read several arguments in favor of early toilet training. They train early in Europe! Toddlers are more compliant than three-year-olds! Diapers are bad for the environment! You may even read published studies concluding that children who train later are more likely to end up with incontinence or overactive bladders. There's just one flaw in this research: The authors never checked, via X-ray, to see if these kids were constipated at the time they started training. The records we keep at my clinic suggest that among late trainers, it's not the age of training but rather unrecognized constipation that correlates with problems. We have found that children who trained after age three and have toileting troubles either trained late *because* they were constipated (their parents had tried earlier but failed) or trained late *and* are constipated. There is no way that healthy, developmentally normal, unconstipated children who learn to use the potty at three and a half have a higher rate of chronic pee or poop accidents than children who train at two and a half. It's simply impossible. Every year of constipation-free, uninhibited voiding (in other words, wearing diapers) leads to bladder growth; every year of holding shrinks the bladder and makes it more overactive. I challenge anyone to prove otherwise.

On the other hand, plenty of kids who train as toddlers—including healthy, constipation-free toddlers—often end up with significant bladder and bowel problems. I'm not saying that children who potty train at a young age are destined to have troubles, but I believe they are at much higher risk than the kids who stay in diapers longer. In my experience it's best to keep the decision of when to pee or poop out of a child's hands for as long as possible. Now, I understand that at some point most parents tire of changing diapers, and having three or four kids in diapers at once is a huge pain. But then again so is bringing your child to an appointment with me. I welcome any proponent of early toilet training to spend a day with me in my clinic. It will be a real eye-opener.

What does all this have to do with schools? Well, a huge number of preschools require their students to be toilet trained—no pull-ups allowed—by age three. This was the policy at the Arlington, Virginia, public Montessori program that suspended Zoe Rosso for having too many accidents, and it's common among preschools where the starting age is three. It is less common among programs that offer preschool in addition to day care for younger toddlers and/or babies. Because of these policies countless parents, facing a September dryness deadline, start training their children before the kids show the key signs of readiness. When is a child ready? When she can tell you she is peeing and pooping, when she asks to use the toilet, and when she can dress and undress herself. Many parents, rightfully worried about trying to cram in potty training and preferring to give their children ample time to master potty skills, start well in advance of the child's three-year-old birthday. I've already told you how that can turn out.

But in case you missed it elsewhere in the book, I'll say it again. For kids who trained before they were developmentally ready or who were constipated at the time they were trained, the pressure to stay dry at school, without the safety net of a pull-up, only makes problems worse. Think about it: You're placing a three-year-old in an unfamiliar environment where, for possibly the first time in his life, he has no family members around for half the day, and you're expecting him to interrupt his teacher during the story circle and announce that he needs to use the toilet or to climb out of the fort he's just built with his friends and make his way over to the potty. Whoever thought that was a good idea has surely never set foot in a pediatric urology clinic.

What happens is that the child doesn't go, because she feels too inhibited or excited or worried that some other kid will take the puzzle she was playing with, and she develops an overactive bladder, a clogged rectum, or both. That seems to be what happened to Zoe Rosso, who probably was constipated before starting preschool and was too shy to let her teachers know when she felt the urge to go. Though she is no longer constipated and her accidents have greatly diminished, even now, at four and a half, Zoe is reluctant to speak up in class when she needs to use the bathroom. Her folks still struggle to persuade her that listening to her body is her top priority. Children who attend schools with "toilet trained by three" policies may end up with a stellar command of the alphabet and know six words that rhyme with *tree*, but many of these kids are totally ill-equipped to deal with the smelly bathrooms and restrictive policies that await them in elementary school and beyond. These kids are being set up for catastrophe.

According to a letter issued by the Arlington Public Schools' Office of Early Childhood Education, Zoe's school insisted upon a temporary period of withdrawal to allow the Rossos to "work more closely" with Zoe and give her "more one-on-one, at-home attention" so that she could master potty training and return to school. But Zoe Rosso didn't need more attention. She needed a high dose of laxatives, followed by a regimented voiding schedule, medication, and physical therapy. With an undetected mass of poop in her rectum, there was simply no way for her to stay dry. Expecting her to try only put more strain on her overtaxed bladder.

Preschools like Zoe's attempt to justify their policies as staffing issues. The Arlington Public School System issued a letter stating that its Montessori program, which reserves two thirds of it spots for low-income families, is staffed at a student-teacher ratio of twenty-three to two, similar to its kindergarten classrooms. "Because we want to maximize participation in our programs, it has always been our policy that children must be toilet trained," the letter stated. "Lowering our student-to-staff ratio to accommodate potty training would significantly reduce the number of children we can serve."

It's admirable that the Arlington Public School System wants to serve as many children as possible, but what kind of service are they, and similar programs, giving to the children who do attend? Developmentally, preschool-age children are a lot different from kindergarteners. Children who are newly potty trained need a lot of follow-up, no matter how well they are able to stay dry. They need frequent reminders to use the toilet, and they need teachers who make sure each child does use the toilet every two hours or so. Truly this is more important than making sure they competently can use scissors or paint with watercolors. The Arlington Public School System maintains that with a twenty-three to two student-teacher ratio, they can't possibly give attention to toileting issues. My point exactly! They need to change the ratio or simply allow kids to wear pull-up diapers, not enforce arbitrary rules on three-year-olds.

In my opinion preschools and camps for preschool-age kids should not have toilet-training requirements. Allowing preschoolers to wear pull-ups is not going to ruin anyone's preschool class or summer camp, especially since kids this age typically can change their own clothes without disrupting the class. Perhaps you are thinking: *When will it end? We'll have kindergarteners in diapers!* But at some point, usually by their fourth birthday, all children are self-conscious about wearing pull-ups, and their parents are embarrassed, too. Peer pressure almost always takes care of the issue. We don't need school principals stepping in as enforcers.

The Rossos tried to get the policy changed at Zoe's school. They did not succeed. But they also didn't have all the facts about Zoe's condition, and neither did the school system. When I contacted the Arlington Public School System, the director of Early Childhood and Elementary Education said she could not comment on the Rosso case "due to confidentiality issues." She also stated that students who have documented medical conditions and/or disabilities are not excluded because of such issues and "are provided reasonable accommodations to enable them to participate in Arlington Public School System services and programs." That might help a child whose doctor has recognized that a child's urinary problems are related to constipation and who has prescribed treatment for that child. But it's not going to help the majority of kids with toileting problems, whose problems are unrecognized and untreated, or the kids whose problems are triggered or exacerbated by the age-three deadline and no-pull-up policy.

If you encounter a preschool that won't let a three-year-old wear pull-ups, bring in a copy of this book. If the administrators are still not persuaded that their policy is misguided, have them call me! If they won't, find a different school. You will save your family from much frustration and anxiety in the long run.

IF YOU ARE DETERMINED TO
POTTY TRAIN YOUR CHILD EARLY

I don't believe in toilet training children for the purpose of meeting the requirements for a summer camp or preschool or because Mom and Dad are tired of changing diapers. I believe in potty training when kids are ready—when they show an interest and can tell you when they are peeing or pooping—and I believe that few kids are genuinely ready before age three. (Some toddlers with older siblings insist that they want to use the potty, like their brother or sister, but often they don't understand what that means.) Nonetheless I'm sure some children younger than age three truly are ready to toilet train, just as some kids are way ahead of the curve for other milestones, whether it's walking, talking, or riding a bike. If you feel certain your child is among them, or if you are absolutely set on sending your child to a school that requires three-year-olds to be trained, following is my advice for doing all you can to preempt problems:

• *Make sure your child's poops are mushy before you start training.* I mean *mush*, like numbers 4, 5, or 6 on the Bristol Stool

Toileting Problems: The School-Age Years

Back when I was in school, we were bombarded with health presentations. We had routine spine checks for scoliosis, and we had dental-health awareness weeks—we'd have to chew those red capsules that stain the plaque on your teeth to show

Scale (see Figure 2-1 on page 37). I'm talking mashed sweet potatoes or hummus. The sure way to sabotage the process is to try to toilet train a constipated kid. If your child's poops are formed, like logs or pebbles, or become formed during the toilet-training process, your child is constipated, and you should read Chapter 2 and get her pooping chocolate pudding for several months before you attempt training.

• *Watch your child like a Secret Service agent once he is out of diapers.* (This applies to all newly trained kids, regardless of when they trained.) Have him on a peeing schedule so that he never goes more than about two hours without using the toilet. Have him sit on the potty to poop after breakfast and dinner. Never ask, "Do you need to go potty?" All kids will say no. It's your job to instruct your child to go. Never, ever lose track of the last time he pooped and what his poop looked like.

• *Keep an eye out for signs of developing problems.* The potty dance isn't cute or funny; it means your child is holding. So does sprinting to the bathroom. You need to nip these problems in the bud, no matter what your child's school policy requires.

how lousy you are at brushing. And, of course, we had sex education. But not once did anyone check to see if we felt comfortable using our school bathrooms or let us know how important it is to pee or poop in a timely manner. Little has changed. These days schools have Children's Mental Health Awareness

Week, Obesity Awareness Week, Drug Awareness Week, and Sleep Awareness Week. Heck, Virginia public schools even have Rabies Awareness Week.

Let me tell you: A lot more kids develop medical problems from holding pee and poop than get bit by rabid dogs.

Not only are we failing to teach kids about healthy elimination habits, but with restrictive policies and practices, such as limited bathroom passes during class time, and the persistent neglect of school bathroom conditions, we actually are achieving the opposite. One of my favorite research studies, published in the *Journal of Urology*, had this title: "Do public schools teach voiding dysfunction?" Yes, they do! In this survey of Iowa elementary school teachers, 80 percent reported that students were assigned set times for bathroom breaks. One third of the teachers admitted asking a child requesting a bathroom pass to wait. A paltry *15* percent suspected an underlying health problem in children who peed or pooped in their pants. Forty-two percent noticed bullying in the boys' bathrooms.

And this was in elementary school! You generally don't find seven-year-olds ripping off stall doors, spray painting erotic graffiti on the mirrors, or hurling wet paper towels at their peers for going number two. And that's the least of what goes on at many middle schools and high schools. At one school in Georgia, students were caught having sex in the bathroom. The school's solution? Lock most of the bathrooms. Good going! That may have stopped the bathroom sex, but it also forced 1,200 kids to use the few toilets in the cafeteria. At another school students were messing with the toilet paper, so the principal's answer was to remove toilet tissue from the stalls and have teachers stand outside the bathrooms handing out piles of TP to students who asked. Though I sympathize with desperate administrators, I can tell you that my patients aren't about to discuss with their teachers how much toilet paper they need. They're going to bypass the bathroom altogether.

You can't blame school restroom conditions entirely on misbehaving students, misguided reactions by administrators, or toilet-paper shortages. The architecture itself can doom the students. At some schools the bathrooms are designed like airport restrooms, with doorless entryways. That may work well for restrooms frequented by adults with carry-on luggage and the children they are supervising—restrooms where people generally aim to pee in the toilets and are more interested in catching their flights than tormenting the guy in the next stall over. But at your average high school with doorless entries, the stench from the clogged toilets and urine puddles on the floor wafts out into the hallway, grossing out students who might otherwise have considered relieving themselves. Plus, the easy access scares off many girls, who know that boys don't even have to open a door to sneak a peek.

I've only scratched the icky surface of the bathroom problems that plague so many of our public schools. You can read more about these problems and concrete suggestions to solve them at Project CLEAN's website, projectclean.us.

What Parents Can Do

In a survey conducted on nearly five hundred students from seven Milwaukee, Wisconsin, public high schools, six out of seven students said they believed sanitation in their bathrooms was "poor." Not a single student stated that his bathroom conditions were even "good," let alone "very good." Those are worse ratings than *Daddy Day Care* earned. (No, I didn't see the movie, despite the heavy emphasis on jokes about bodily functions.) What's going on at middle schools and high schools is nothing short of a public health disaster. And there's no equivalent of Federal Emergency Management Agency to coordinate relief. In most regions, state and local health agencies aren't watching out for your kid's bathrooms, either.

In fact, fewer than a half a dozen states even have laws requiring school bathrooms to be clean, and enforcement of these laws is not a priority. The handful of states that do have laws, including California, Pennsylvania, and Florida, provide a glimpse into just how crummy conditions are. In Sarasota County, Florida, more than one third of the schools were cited for health code violations in a single year because of their bathrooms. Imagine what goes on in the school bathrooms that never even get inspected by a governmental authority. Other than complying with state engineering and plumbing codes and mandated toilet-to-student ratios, the vast majority of the country's nearly one million public school bathrooms don't have to meet any standards for cleanliness. Legally they can be completely, totally gross.

I didn't know any of this before I spoke with Dr. Keating and started researching school bathroom issues myself. Dr. Keating, who earned his doctorate in education policy and has served as a teacher, education lobbyist, and school-board member, launched Project CLEAN in 1996 after hearing bathroom horror stories from his son and daughter and watching a neighbor boy sprint across his lawn every afternoon after holding all day at school. Dr. Keating has visited thousands of school bathrooms at hundreds of schools in some two dozen states and several foreign countries, including Ireland and India, where he attended World Toilet Organization summits. He has trained teenagers to write restroom work orders, inspired football players to rap about flushing, spearheaded school science projects on hand washing, introduced custodians and students to one another, and awarded art students for their posters reminding boys to improve their aim. My favorite: "Don't miss or the custodian you'll diss." See this marvelous poster on page 151, and read about the dean of students who spearheaded the project on page 150. Dr. Keating has persuaded schools to hold assemblies on toilet etiquette, install graffiti-proof doors, and change bathroom signage from BOYS and GIRLS to MEN and WOMEN, boosting pride and respect among students. He is dogged in his efforts, creative in his solutions, and astoundingly knowledgeable about germ-detection technology, school politics, and what makes thirteen-year-old boys care about keeping the stalls clean. He's my hero. Dr. Keating has no shortage of advice on how to improve school bathrooms, and he'll give you ideas if you give him a call, which I recommend you do. (His phone number is on his website.) Here is his advice for parents who want to make a difference.

- *Gear up for the long haul.* Many principals don't want to deal with bathroom issues because they think the problems are unsolvable and because, understandably, they're too busy with about a thousand other agenda items. So parents need to drive the efforts. Just one problem: Parents are often reluctant to make a fuss; they fear being branded "difficult" and worry their children will suffer consequences at school. Don't duck this issue because of school politics! "Change only happens if schools are pressured," Dr. Keating notes. "You have to get more than one parent involved and be invested for the long haul. When the principal says, 'I don't have any money,' you have to get off the canvas, just like Rocky." You also need to volunteer to help solve the problem rather than simply rely on the school to take action.

- *Tour the bathrooms.* Next time you're at school for a play or basketball game, wander into the bathrooms. Not just the restrooms near the entrance—those are the ones kept the cleanest to impress parents, according to Dr. Keating. Find the bathrooms down the hall on the third floor (get permission, if necessary) and inspect them using Dr. Keating's "four senses" inspection approach: look, listen, smell, and feel. (Not to worry about using that fifth sense; there's nothing you need to taste in the bathroom. Whew!) Inspect the back of the door for graffiti, look up at the lighting, glance down to see whether the drain is clogged. Close your eyes and listen for the sound of any running toilets or leaky sinks. Take a whiff. Flush the urinals and press the soap dispenser. Take notes and, if it's allowed, take pictures with your cell phone. Then report any problems to the principal in detail. Inspect both the boys' and girls' bathrooms, so grab a companion of the opposite gender.

- *Make bathroom cleanliness a PTA issue.* Become a member of your school's parent-teacher association, whether it's the PTA, PTO, or PTSA, and find out if a building and grounds committee exists. If so, ask to create a subcommittee on bathrooms, and schedule a meeting with the principal. Tell her you'd like to discuss the missing stall doors in the second-floor bathroom or toilet-paper brackets that have become unhinged. Stay on her. If the principal says, "We've put in a requisition and we hope to get new ones soon," find out the definition of *soon*. And so on.

- *If the PTA route doesn't fly, find another structure.* Many states have laws mandating school-improvement councils made up of local residents. Also, a section in the Healthy, Hunger-Free Kids Act (Public Law 111-296, section 204) requires every school district in the country to have a wellness policy to "promote student health and reduce childhood obesity." As a result many school districts have created wellness councils. Though these councils tend to focus on the two *es*—eating and exercise—as Dr. Keating points out, certainly the third *e*, elimination, falls under the umbrella of "student health."

  In addition to pushing for clean, safe restrooms, advocate for policies that allow kids to use the restrooms whenever they need to, not just during the four minutes between biology and algebra. Patients tell me all the time that they are limited to a certain number of bathroom passes per term; once they've used them up—well, tough luck! Administrators may insist on pass limits because some kids abuse the "privilege" of using the bathroom, but punishing the many for the crimes of the few only invites serious health problems and resentment from students. Until change happens at your child's school, get a doctor's note for your child stating that she must be allowed to use the bathroom whenever she wants. If your child is too afraid or grossed out by the bathrooms, have the doctor add that she must be allowed to use the faculty restrooms. "A doctor's note will override school policies," says Dee Carter, the mother of my UTI patient Cici and an elementary school reading teacher. "Teachers have to abide by them."

- *Get students and staff fired up.* Your own child may not be jazzed to join Mom or Dad in efforts to clean up toilets, but no doubt other students will want to take up the cause. Find a club on campus that concerns citizenship, community service, or school improvement. Form a committee that involves students, teachers, parents, and the custodian and meet once a month, brainstorming until you come up with a plan. It's important for students to know that the adults at school—the principals, teachers, custodians, nurses, and counselors—care enough to follow through. "It all comes down to respect," Dr. Keating says. "Kids have to respect their school restrooms as if they were their own, and faculty, staff, and administration have to respect the students as young adults who can be trusted to take care of their basic, biological needs in an acceptable setting."

- *Get creative with your team.* Hold an adopt-a-bathroom contest, assigning school clubs to renovate and decorate bathrooms, and have students write essays or perform skits about school bathrooms. (Check out "The Making of the Skit 'True Dat'" on projectclean.us for a wonderful example of a creative teacher and kids improving middle-school restrooms.) Establish a whistle-blowing system so students can report incidents of bathroom shenanigans to a designated staff member without fear of retribution from other students. Announce all this in an assembly that also explains the serious health consequences of holding pee and poop. Of course my dream would be for every school in America to hold Toileting Awareness Week, but at this point I'd settle for eliminating bathroom-pass limits. My best advice: Get your school to bring in Dr. Keating. He'll blow everyone's minds with the sheer number of great ideas he has.

The Topic No One Wants to Talk About

Every time a new elementary school is built, shiny new signs go up—LIBRARY, CAFETERIA, PRINCIPAL—but often, the bathrooms are overlooked. As Dr. Keating points out, the absence of signage speaks loudly: "This isn't a subject to talk about." That's precisely what Dr. Sean O'Regan, back in Chapter 1, told me when I asked why he thought his ground-breaking research in the 1980s generated so little interest, even among urologists. And it is the reason so many children end up in my office after their problems had gone unrec-ognized literally for years. I cannot emphasize this enough: Talk to your child about how often—or if—he is using the bathroom at school. Every day I meet parents who had no clue that their child was too afraid or revolted to pee or poop between the hours of eight and three. Ask your kid, "Did you have soap today in the bathroom?" If he says, "I don't know— I didn't use it," you know you have a problem.

BATHROOM CLEANUP:
ONE SCHOOL'S SUCCESS STORY

What makes students treat their school's bathrooms with respect? Meeting their custodian, for starters.

As part of a restroom-improvement initiative at Glennwood 4-5 Academy in Decatur, Georgia, Dean of Students Rodney Thomas introduced one of the school's custodians to the student body, one classroom at a time.

"I said, 'This is Miss Pat. It is not her job to flush the toilets, clean your poop off the walls, and pick paper towels off the floor. How would you feel if you had to do that?'" recalls Mr. Thomas.

The students, all fourth and fifth graders, were so moved that they wrote cards to Miss Pat, apologizing and promising to do better. When they'd see her in the hall, they'd say, "Hey, Miss Pat, how are you doing?"

Meeting Miss Pat was just one part of the bathroom project, led by Mr. Thomas and Dr. Tom Keating of Project CLEAN (see page 133). Mr. Thomas admits that when the school's principal assigned him to the project, he hadn't considered his school's bathrooms to be a problem, and he had no idea that huge percentages of students avoid peeing or pooping at school.

"When I heard 'bathrooms,' I thought: *Please, we have the weight of the world on us. We have to deal with test scores and dismissal procedures and lunchroom monitoring and conduct on the buses—on and on.* But then I saw how bathrooms tie into a school's culture and academic success."

Compared to the district's middle schools and high schools, Glennwood, which served only fourth and fifth graders (and now is a K–3 school), had relatively mild bathroom problems. Still, kids didn't always flush, paper towels littered the floors, graffiti was scrawled in a few places, and the restrooms had a faint stench of urine.

"Dr. Keating pointed out that the lack of respect now would lead to much bigger problems at the middle school level," Mr. Thomas says.

So they held short classroom talks and an all-school assembly. Dr. Keating talked about hygiene. The librarian presented the classic book, *Everybody Poops*. "We wanted to make respecting the bathroom and not being embarrassed about poop a way of life," Mr. Thomas says. "The kids embraced it. It became a lively, fun conversation."

The school addressed bathroom design flaws, too. They replaced sink fixtures that were difficult for the kids to turn off. They secured a urinal for a boys' bathroom that had only toilets. They replaced dull, computer-generated posters with posters created by students in an all-school art contest.

"The kids loved seeing their artwork on the walls," Mr. Thomas says. "It gave them a sense of pride. I never saw any of those posters on the floor, unlike the other posters."

Soon, the kids were policing themselves, Mr. Thomas says. "They'd come up to me or Miss Pat and say, 'So-and-so left the water running,' or 'Someone pooped and didn't flush.'"

The effects of the project were lasting, Mr. Thomas reports. "The kids went on to middle school with the mind-set that you have to respect the bathrooms, and now those middle-school bathrooms are a lot cleaner than they used to be."

My goal isn't to bash our nation's schools. I know many teachers and administrators, from the preschool level through high school, and I speak to them about these issues. I know what they are up against and that they care deeply about their students. I'm simply trying to raise awareness for an expensive and serious epidemic that is completely preventable. Preschool policies that mandate potty training by age three, along with our public school system's tolerance for empty soap dispensers and restrictions on bathroom passes, are causing medical problems in otherwise healthy children. We need to work together to fix this problem.

CHAPTER 8

Nutrition for Super Pooping

I once had to sign a contract promising that I would not feed my children any more Pop-Tarts. The person who forced me to sign this document was my wife. I'd gotten busted one morning when our oldest daughter, then three, blurted out, "Strawberry Pop-Tarts are my favorite!" I had specifically instructed her to keep quiet about the treat, but apparently three-year-olds can't be trusted with classified information.

Let's face it: Most children love junk food, and parents love making their kids happy. It's the rare kindergartener who will choose a banana over a brownie or mini cucumbers over corn chips. Nonetheless, every day I see patients whose junked-out diets are making their potty problems worse or preventing a full recovery. If your child's wetting issues are caused by constipation—and most childhood urinary problems are—unclogging her colon with laxatives and the other strategies described in Chapter 2 is only half the battle. Keeping her insides clear, with high-fiber foods and plenty of water, is just as important, especially over the long-term. So what your child eats for breakfast, nibbles for lunch, or sips after soccer practice matters a lot.

Every once in a while, I see patients who have become severely constipated despite stellar eating habits. Mom swears the child's favorite food is broccoli and that the kid eats nothing but fruits, vegetables, and bean salads, and I believe them. Some kids are genetically or temperamentally prone to constipation no matter how well they eat. But the reality is most kids have crummy diets. They may go days without eating a single fruit or vegetable, they guzzle soda, and their meals come almost entirely from a box, which generally means the foods are high in saturated and trans fat and seriously lacking in fiber.

To give you an idea of how poorly American kids eat, consider: Preschoolers need at least 14 grams of fiber a day, yet 88 percent of American children ages two to five fail to meet that goal.[16] Almost nine out of ten kids! One study, conducted at the Ohio State University College of Medicine, found that constipated children were averaging less than one fourth of the recommended fiber intake—and that was back when daily fiber recommendations were lower than they are today.[17] That's a recipe for hard, painful poops.

I know families rely heavily on fast food because of busy schedules, but high-fiber foods can be quick and easy as well. And 14 grams of fiber is not such a tall order. To meet this

16   Kranz S, Mitchell DC, Siega-Riz AM, Smiciklas-Wright H. Dietary fiber intake by American preschoolers is associated with more nutrient-dense diets. *Am Diet Assoc.* Feb 2005;105(2):221-5.

17   McClung HJ, Boyne L, Heitlinger L. Constipation and dietary fiber intake in children. *Pediatrics.* Nov 1995;96(5 Pt 2):999–1000.

recommendation you don't have to plant an organic vegetable garden and live off of it! A kid could meet the mark with a cup of Post Raisin Bran (8 grams) topped with a sliced banana (3 grams) for breakfast and a small apple (3.5 grams) for a snack. Or, a Baja Fresh Mini Bean and Cheese Burrito (11 grams) and a tangerine (3 grams) or a cup of strawberries (also 3 grams). As my wife likes to point out to me: Hey, it's not that tough. And yet kids across America are starting the day with Trix Fruitalicious Swirls (zero fiber) and apple juice (virtually no fiber) and snacking on fruit roll-ups (yes, zero, even when made with "real" fruit). Zero + zero + zero = zero!

No doubt, Pop-Tart–loving dads like me are contributing to the problem. So for this chapter I've enlisted nutritionist Meredith Carter Conley, R.D., L.D.N, a dietitian in Nashville, Tennessee, who has worked with many constipated children. We explain how eating more fiber and drinking more water can help your child poop better, and we offer tricks for sneaking more fruits, veggies, and whole grains into your child's lunch box and making healthy eating fun. We also answer questions such as: How do I know if my child is eating enough fiber? Which kid-friendly foods have the most fiber? What if the only four food groups my child will touch are french fries, chicken nuggets, pizza, and hamburgers?

Why Fiber Helps Your Kid Poop

When you eat an apple, most of it is digested by your stomach, absorbed by your small intestine, and then converted to energy, so you can do things like walk, talk, and stay awake while reading this book. But parts of that apple are not digestible. Those parts are the fiber, which—stay with me here—comes in two varieties. Soluble fiber is found in the fleshy, pulpy interior of fruits, veggies, beans, and other plant foods. Insoluble fiber is found in the husks and peels, like the stringy membranes of an orange, the tiny seeds of a black-berry, and that thin peel on each kernel of corn. Soluble fiber keeps poop soft and slimy, by absorbing water and binding with fat. Insoluble fiber adds bulk to your poop. Research shows that the more fiber you eat, the heftier your poops, the faster your poop travels through the colon, and the better the laxative effect. Yes, there are researchers who have devoted their careers to weighing people's poops and tracking how long said poops take to exit. Fun stuff!

Fiber is found in all plant foods, such as fruits, veggies, beans, peas, nuts, and seeds. It's also found in grains—but only in whole grains, such as barley, oats, quinoa, and brown rice, not in refined grains, like white rice and Fruity Pebbles cereal, which have had the fiber almost entirely stripped. (Inciden-tally, not only is the fiber stripped but most of the vitamins and minerals are, too.) Likewise, there's lots of fiber in an apple or an orange but very little in apple juice or orange juice. While fiber-rich foods help poop move along, toaster pastries and french fries do the opposite. Fats can slow digestion, and any time your child fills up on chicken nuggets and fries, he's miss-ing out on an opportunity to bulk up his poop with fruits, veg-etables, beans, and whole grains. And the more sugary foods a kid eats, the less room he has for nutritious, fiber-rich foods.

Plus, children who eat too much sugar are more likely to be overweight and inactive, which has an indirect effect on promoting constipation.

How Much Fiber Your Child Needs

Your child's daily fiber requirement depends on her age, size, and activity level. Bigger, more active kids need more calories and therefore more fiber. The U.S. Government's latest Dietary Guidelines for Americans recommend 14 grams of fiber for each 1,000 calories consumed (this applies to children and adults).[18] Here's how much fiber your child needs each day based on the government's guidelines.

Child's Age	Recommended Fiber Intake (grams)
2–3	14
4–8	17–20
9–13	22–25
14–18	25–31

How Fluids Help Your Child Poop

When it comes to stellar pooping, fiber isn't the only nutritional consideration; fluids are key, too. Fluid helps poop move through the intestines, so if your child isn't drinking enough water with his shredded wheat and blueberries, all that fiber could essentially act as cement.

---

18 www.cnpp.usda.gov/Publications/DietaryGuidelines/2010/PolicyDoc/Chapter4.pdf.

Many foods that are high in fiber also are loaded with water. For example, vegetables are 85 to 90 percent water. Hot cereal is about 85 percent water. (Potato chips, FYI, are only 2 percent water.) But the water your child gets from food isn't enough. She also needs to drink plenty of fluids. See the chart opposite for your child's daily fluid needs. She needs substantially more when the weather is hot or she's playing sports or doing other physical activity.

Does the fluid your child drinks have to be water? No, milk is great, too. What if your child prefers juice, punch, or lemonade? Those drinks contain plenty of water, but they also have little or no nutritional value and lots of calories. Plus sweetened beverages contribute to tooth decay. So know that other drinks count, but aim for your child to drink mostly water.

One option is to flavor the water with a slice or two of orange or lemon or mix in a small bit of fruit juice. Some kids will drink more water if you give them a straw. Some are motivated by water bottles with their favorite cartoon characters.

It may take some work to help your child meet his fluid needs. These days most school-age children don't have much opportunity to drink. Let's say your child spends nine to ten hours sleeping, another hour (or more, depending on bus schedules) getting to and from school, and another five or so hours in the classroom. You may be surprised at how little fluid your child is consuming! Plus most kids just aren't that interested in drinking.

Your Child's Fluid Needs

The U.S. government doesn't have guidelines for fluid intake, but here's an estimate based on a formula used to give hospitalized children enough IV fluids to stay hydrated.[19] These guidelines are for total fluid intake, and since food contains some fluid, the figures somewhat overestimate how much fluid kids need to drink.

Child's Weight	Recommended Fluid Intake
30 pounds	38 ounces
40 pounds	46 ounces
50 pounds	51 ounces
60 pounds	54 ounces

Scoring Your Kid's Fiber Intake

Quick: How many grams of fiber is your kid eating a day? Six? Twelve? Twenty?

Chances are, you have no idea. Life is busy enough without running around adding up fiber grams. But if you don't know your child's starting point, you won't know how much of a change he needs to make, whether just a little tweaking or more of an overhaul.

So let's do some tallying. Fill in the Three-Day Food and Fluid Log starting on page 162, recording every morsel your

---

19   Feng WC, Churchill BM. Dysfunctional elimination syndrome in children without obvious spinal cord diseases. *Pediatric Clinics of North America.* Dec 2001;48(6):1489–1504.

child eats and every juice box or cup of water she sips—well, as accurately as you possibly can, since you may not know exactly what she's eating at school or at a playdate. Include at least one weekday and one weekend day, since our eating patterns often change on weekends. Make careful notes about the amount your child consumes. You can find the fiber content on packaged foods by looking at the Nutrition Facts label. Most fast-food and restaurant chains post their menu item's nutrition information, including fiber content, on their websites. For foods that aren't packaged, like an apple or slice of pizza, go to the U.S. Department of Agriculture's (USDA) Nutrient Database for Standard Reference at nal.usda.gov/fnic/foodcomp/search/. You'll probably have to do some guesswork—it may be tough to estimate the fiber content of your enchilada casserole, but three days of logging should give you a ballpark sense of your child's fiber intake. We've included a sample log page to help you get started.

How did your child's fiber stats rate? If your child is off the mark, give the rest of this chapter a good read and start slowly ratcheting up his daily fiber intake, by 3 or 4 grams a week. *Slowly* is the operative word. If your child's fiber consumption goes from zero to sixty in two days, you will have one unhappy camper, with stomach cramping, bloating, and possibly diarrhea.

Foods with Lots of Fiber

A while back, researchers at Penn State University asked the parents of five thousand preschoolers what their children ate over a two-day period. They were trying to find out how much fiber the kids consumed and what foods the fiber was coming from. Not only was the children's fiber intake far below the government's recommendation, but what little fiber the children did eat came from foods that have relatively little fiber to begin with, like applesauce and fruit cocktail. Kids ate such small amounts of high-fiber foods, such as apples, blueberries, raisins, squash, and broccoli, that these foods didn't even contribute to the total fiber estimates.

Boosting your child's fiber intake isn't hard, but you need to know where to look. Keep in mind that two foods with the same amount of fiber aren't necessarily equally good choices. And be on the lookout for tricky marketing intended to persuade you that junk food isn't actually junk food. I'll give you an example using the Pop-Tarts that got me in trouble with my wife. Kellogg's makes a product called Low Fat Frosted Strawberry Toaster Pastries with Whole Grain and Fiber. It has 3 grams of fiber, about the same as a cup of blueberries. Woo hoo! That's about 3 grams more than you'll get in a Frosted Blueberry Pop-Tart. But sadly that doesn't make those low-fat, fiber-added toasted pastries a terrific choice. They're also loaded with sugar (three of the first five ingredients are sugar, corn syrup, and dextrose) and have 180 calories—and no strawberries. That cup of juicy blueberries contains just 80 calories, has no added sugar, and is rich in substances that help prevent cancer, improve memory, and do other amazing things.

The best fiber sources are those that don't come in packages and that look pretty much the same on the tree or the vine or in the ground as they do in the supermarket. (Do potato chips look

THREE-DAY FOOD AND FLUID LOG

SAMPLE *Day 1:* Monday

Breakfast	Amount of Food or Drink:	Fiber (g)	Fluid (oz)
1 cup Trix		1	
Skim milk			8
1 scrambled egg			
Orange juice			4

Snack	Amount of Food or Drink:	Fiber (g)	Fluid (oz)
1 cheese stick			

Lunch	Amount of Food or Drink:	Fiber (g)	Fluid (oz)
Ham and cheese on white bread			
1 oz Fritos		1	
1 pudding cup			
1 juice pouch			6

Snack	Amount of Food or Drink:	Fiber (g)	Fluid (oz)
Ice cream sandwich			

Dinner	Amount of Food or Drink:	Fiber (g)	Fluid (oz)
Meatloaf			
Egg noodles			
1/2 cup carrots		3	
Apple juice			8

Snack	Amount of Food or Drink:	Fiber (g)	Fluid (oz)
1 package fruit snacks			

Totals: ___5___ (g) ___26___ (oz)

THREE-DAY FOOD AND FLUID LOG

Day 1: _____

Breakfast	Amount of Food or Drink:	Fiber (g)	Fluid (oz)

Snack	Amount of Food or Drink:	Fiber (g)	Fluid (oz)

Lunch	Amount of Food or Drink:	Fiber (g)	Fluid (oz)

Snack	Amount of Food or Drink:	Fiber (g)	Fluid (oz)

Dinner	Amount of Food or Drink:	Fiber (g)	Fluid (oz)

Snack	Amount of Food or Drink:	Fiber (g)	Fluid (oz)

Totals: _____(g)   _____(oz)

Day 2: _____

Breakfast	Amount of Food or Drink:	Fiber (g)	Fluid (oz)

Snack	Amount of Food or Drink:	Fiber (g)	Fluid (oz)

Lunch	Amount of Food or Drink:	Fiber (g)	Fluid (oz)

Snack	Amount of Food or Drink:	Fiber (g)	Fluid (oz)

Dinner	Amount of Food or Drink:	Fiber (g)	Fluid (oz)

Snack	Amount of Food or Drink:	Fiber (g)	Fluid (oz)

Totals: _____(g) _____(oz)

Day 3: _____

Breakfast	Amount of Food or Drink:	Fiber (g)	Fluid (oz)

Snack	Amount of Food or Drink:	Fiber (g)	Fluid (oz)

Lunch	Amount of Food or Drink:	Fiber (g)	Fluid (oz)

Snack	Amount of Food or Drink:	Fiber (g)	Fluid (oz)

Dinner	Amount of Food or Drink:	Fiber (g)	Fluid (oz)

Snack	Amount of Food or Drink:	Fiber (g)	Fluid (oz)

Totals: _____(g) _____(oz)

anything like potatoes? Nope.) You'll encounter more high-fiber foods if you shop the perimeter of grocery stores rather than the center aisles. One exception are frozen fruits and veggies, which are just as nutritious as fresh but often are less expensive and, of course, longer lasting. When you do buy packaged foods, such as breads, grains, and pastas, look for those with a short list of ingredients, ideally ones you can pronounce. Fewer ingredients generally means a product is closer to the form in which it came out of the ground, with more nutritious stuff and fiber remaining and less unhealthy stuff added. Post Shredded Wheat cereal, for example, contains two ingredients (whole-grain wheat and a preservative called BHT). Blueberry Pop-Tarts have forty-one ingredients, including four different incarnations of sugar (corn syrup, high fructose corn syrup, dextrose, and, oh yeah, sugar).

Teach your child to make savvy fiber choices, too. The older your child, the more important it is that she knows how to make good choices herself. You're not always there to oversee what she's eating, and even when you are, you don't want to get locked into a power struggle. Later in this chapter we provide tips on getting your child to eat healthfully without pressuring her.

The next section helps you make the best choices in the main food categories that contain fiber.

NUTRITION TIDBIT

Children consume more than half of their fruit intake as juice, yet juice has virtually no fiber.

SOURCE: 2010 USDA DIETARY GUIDELINES

Fruits

Most kids love sweet things, so fruits are the easiest high-fiber foods to pack into a child's diet. Fresh and frozen are both great choices. Avoid buying fruits canned in syrup; look for those canned in their own juice. Dried fruits can be great fiber sources—just watch the calories. Many fruit "snacks" and fruit "leathers" are basically just candy. See the chart here for the fiber content of various fruits.

Fruit	Serving	Fiber grams
Raspberries	1 cup	8
Prunes	½ cup	6.2
Pear, with skin	1 medium	5.5
Apple, with skin	1 medium	4.4
Dried apricot halves	½ cup	4.3
Strawberry halves	1¼ cup	3.8
Blueberries	1 cup	3.6
Dates, medjool	5	3.2
Banana	1 medium	3.1
Orange	1 medium	3.1
Pineapple	1 cup chunks	2.3
Peach	1 medium	2.2
Raisins	¼ cup	2.0
Grapes	2 cups	1.6

Vegetables

Veggies have a bad rap—remember when President George H. W. Bush announced to the nation that he didn't like broccoli?—so many parents don't even bother. I was at Costco

GETTING YOUR CHILD TO EAT MORE FRUIT

- Add sliced banana or berries (fresh or microwaved) to your child's breakfast cereal or oatmeal. Let your child do the microwaving.
- Make a fruit smoothie for breakfast or a snack. Rather than use frozen yogurt or sugar-added yogurt, blend frozen fruit with fresh fruit and nonfat milk or soy milk. Keep sliced just-past-ripe bananas in the freezer and ready to go. They add lots of sweetness and a creamy texture.
- For a treat serve cut-up fruit topped with flavored yogurt or dipped in chocolate, or have your child layer a fruit-and-yogurt parfait with low-sugar, high-fiber granola.
- Add chopped, dried fruits or shredded apples to your pancake or muffin batter or cookie or bread dough.
- Use a melon baller to make a fruit salad. Kids love fruits shaped like balls.
- Serve baked apples or baked pears for a treat instead of cake or cookies.
- Pack a snack of golden raisins, brown raisins, dried cranberries, and nuts.
- Add sliced apples or bananas to a PB&J sandwich.
- Keep fruit handy in the car for snacks after school or before or after sports and other activities. When they're hungry, they'll eat it!
- Have your child assemble a fruit pizza for a treat. Use a cookie-dough crust, cream cheese sweetened with a bit of sugar and maybe a dash of cinnamon, and lots of fresh fruit.
- Provide fruit for your child to make faces on a plate. She might use blueberries for the eyes, kiwi slices for the ears, a strawberry for the nose, peach slices for the mouth, and so on.

recently when a young girl walked by a VitaMix smoothie demonstration featuring pineapple, orange, spinach, kale, and about twenty other kinds of produce and asked her mom if she could try it. The mom said, "Oh, you won't like it—it has vegetables."

Don't emulate that mom! Take the attitude that your child will like veggies, at least some of them, some of the time. See the chart here for some high-fiber options.

Vegetable	Serving	Fiber grams
Avocado	½	6.8
Jicama	1 cup slices	5.9
Artichoke, cooked	1/2	5.1
Spinach	1 cup cooked	4.3
Brussels sprouts	1 cup	4.1
Beets	1 cup	3.8
Potato, with skin, baked	1 medium	3.8
Sweet potato, baked	1 small	3.8
Peas, cooked	1/2 cup	3.0
Green beans	1 cup ½-inch pieces	2.7
Eggplant	1 cup	2.5
Broccoli	1 cup chopped	2.4
Cauliflower	1 cup chopped	2.1
Sweet corn	½ cup kernels	2.1
Green pepper	1 medium	2.0
Cabbage	1 cup shredded	1.8
Carrot, raw	1 medium	1.7

TIPS FOR SNEAKING VEGGIES
INTO YOUR KID'S DIET

- Add small chunks of veggies to spaghetti sauce—your kid won't even notice.
- Go mini! Kids love small things, like miniature sweet peppers, mini-cucumbers, baby carrots, and grape tomatoes.
- Add roasted cauliflower or pureed butternut squash to your mac and cheese.
- Pack your tuna salad with diced cucumber, sweet pepper, red onion, shredded carrots, and sliced grape tomatoes.
- Serve baked sweet potato fries instead of french fries.
- Add shredded zucchini to breads, muffins, and scrambled eggs.
- Take your child to the produce aisle and let him pick out any two vegetables he wants, then go online with him and look for fun ways to prepare them.
- Cut up celery and carrot sticks and provide peanut butter or salsa for dipping.
- Hollow out peppers to use as dipping bowls for hummus.
- Sneak shredded zucchini and yellow squash under the cheese of your homemade pizza. Or offer several veggie toppings and let your child pile them on.

Whole Grains: Pastas, Breads, and Cereals

There's a lot of devious marketing in the grains department. You'll find packages that say, "Made with whole grains," which is like those fruit punches that say, "Made with real fruit." In other words: made with a microscopic amount. You'll find "15-grain bread," with packages of wheat fields waving in the wind, when, in reality, you're eating refined white bread with caramel coloring. Ideally the products you buy should be labeled "100% whole grain." Here are tips for buying grain products.

- For constipated kids, choose cereals with at least 5 grams of fiber per serving. Sorry, Rice Krispies, Corn Pops, and Apple Jacks don't make the cut! (All have no fiber.) Raisin Bran (6 to 8 grams, depending on the brand) is a great choice. Other good options: Cracklin' Oat Bran, All Bran, and GoLean Crunch Original. If your child thinks that high-fiber cereals taste like tree bark, try mixing them into her favorite brand. Note that some super–high-fiber cereals have loads of sugar added to disguise their chalky taste.

- Choose whole-wheat pasta or pasta that is at least 50 percent whole grain.

- Switch from regular English muffins to whole-grain varieties.

- Snack on air-popped popcorn. A three-cup serving contains 3.5 grams of fiber.

- Choose whole-wheat tortillas for quesadillas, enchiladas, soft tacos, and burritos.

- Use whole-wheat flour in your cooking and baking when possible.

NUTRITION TIDBIT

Breakfast cereals advertised to children on TV have 65 percent less fiber and 85 percent more sugar than cereals advertised to adults, according to a report from Yale University's Rudd Center for Food Policy and Obesity. Many popular cereals have as much sugar as a glazed donut. SOURCE: HTTP://CEREALFACTS.ORG/

- Replace white rice with brown rice, wild rice, quinoa, barley, or whole-wheat couscous. If your child resists making the switch, mix the two. One cup of brown rice has 3.5 grams of fiber; white rice has zero.

- Sprinkle wheat germ, ground flaxseed, or bran onto your child's favorite hot or cold cereal or PB&J or into baked goods.

Nuts, Nut Butters, and Seeds

Yes, nuts and nut butters have a lot of calories, so you don't want to give your child unlimited amounts, the way you can with most vegetables. But most kids love PB&J sandwiches, and nuts make a great snack mixed with raisins or dried cranberries. Nut butters and nuts are a great way to get fiber into your child's diet (as long as your child does not have nut allergies, of course). See the chart here for the fiber content of some different nuts and seeds.

Nuts and Seeds	Serving Size	Fiber Grams
Sunflower seeds	¼ cup	3.9
Almonds	1 ounce (23 nuts)	3.5
Almond butter	2 Tbsp	3.2
Soy nut butter	2 Tbsp	3.0
Pistachio nuts	1 ounce (49 nuts)	2.9
Pecans	1 ounce (19 halves)	2.7
Peanut Butter	2 tbsp	2.6
Peanuts	1 ounce	2.5
Flaxseeds	2 tbsp	1.8

Beans, Peas, and Lentils

Beans, peas, and lentils are all in the legume family, but nobody actually uses that word, so let's just call them . . . beans, peas, and lentils. Whatever term you want to use, these are the most fiber rich of all foods. You can add them to pasta salads, soups, casseroles, quesadillas, and tuna salads and dramatically boost the fiber count of your child's lunch or dinner. See the chart here for the fiber content of various legumes.

Legumes	Serving Size	Fiber Grams
Split peas	½ cup	8.1
Lentils	½ cup	7.8
Black beans	½ cup	7.5
Kidney beans	½ cup	6.9
Lima beans	½ cup	6.6
White beans	½ cup	6.3
Refried beans	½ cup	6.0
Pinto beans	½ cup	5.5

NUTRITION TIDBIT

40: Percent of total calories kids consume that are empty calories, like soda, fruit drinks, and desserts.
365: Calories kids get each day from added sugars.
23: Teaspoons of added sugar kids eat each day.

SOURCE: HTTP://RISKFACTOR.CANCER.GOV/DIET/FOODSOURCES/ARTICLE/

TEN BEAN-BASED DISHES
KIDS ACTUALLY LIKE

- Chili with kidney, white, pinto, and/or black beans

- Minestrone soup or lentil soup

- Tacos with black or pinto beans mixed into the meat

- Quesadillas with pinto beans, black beans, or nonfat refried beans

- Tuna salad with white beans or garbanzo beans

- Roasted cinnamon garbanzo beans. A yummy treat!

- Brownies made with black beans. Really! Google it!

- Quinoa salad or corn salad with black beans

- Sweet three-bean salad with green beans, yellow beans, and kidney beans

ARE PRUNES REALLY THE MAGIC BULLET?

More than any other food, prunes and prune juice are known for their laxative effect. Do they really work?

Yes, to some extent, although no amount of prune juice will clear out the kind of hard poop mass that causes wetting problems. Prunes, which kids will like better if you call them "dried plums," are super high in insoluble fiber, the kind that soaks up water. Just five prunes contain almost 3 grams of fiber. They also contain a natural sugar called sorbitol, which soaks up water as well. Most fruits contain small amounts (usually less than 1 percent) of sorbitol, but prunes are about 15 percent sorbitol, which explains why they're such a potent bulking agent.

Kid Meal Makeovers

A few minor changes can make an enormous difference in a child's daily fiber intake. Simply switching from a ham and cheese sandwich on white bread to a PB&J on whole wheat can get your child from zero grams of fiber to (depending on which brand of bread) 10 grams. Adding half an avocado (3.4 grams) and 1/4 cup black beans (3.5 grams) to a quesadilla and using whole-wheat tortillas (5 grams) instead of white gives your child an extra 12 grams of fiber in one meal!

Following is a makeover of the meal listed on the sample page of the Three-Day Food and Fluid Log on page 162.

Before	*After*
Breakfast	**Breakfast**
1 cup Corn Pops	1 cup whole-grain cereal
1 cup skim milk	1 cup skim milk
1 scrambled egg	1 scrambled egg
½ cup orange juice	½ cup blueberries
Snack	**Snack**
1 cheese stick	1 cheese stick
Lunch	**Lunch**
Ham and cheese on white bread	Ham and cheese on whole-wheat bread
1 ounce Fritos	1 ounce Sun Chips
1 pudding cup	1 pudding cup
1 juice pouch	1 small orange
	Water
Snack	**Snack**
Ice cream sandwich	3 cups popcorn
Dinner	**Dinner**
Meatloaf	Meatloaf
Egg noodles	Whole-grain couscous
Carrots	Carrots
Dinner roll	1 cup strawberries
Juice	Water or sugar-free drink
Snack	**Snack**
1 package fruit snacks	Whole-wheat muffin
Estimated fiber: 5 grams	Estimated fiber: 28 grams

FIVE AWESOME BREAKFASTS FOR KIDS

All of these breakfasts have at least 8 grams of fiber, two thirds of a preschooler's needs and nearly half of the 17 to 20 grams recommended for kids ages 4 to 8.

- Half a cup of oatmeal (3 grams) with 1 cup blueberries (4 grams, fresh or frozen), ¼ cup nuts (2 grams), and 1 cup soy milk (1 gram)
- One slice whole-grain toast (4 grams) or whole-grain waffle (pick a brand with at least 4 grams) with 1 tablespoon peanut butter (1.3 grams) and 1 teaspoon honey or preserves; 1 cup frozen mixed berries (3 grams)
- Strawberry-banana smoothie (4 grams: ½ banana, ½ cup frozen strawberries, 1 cup vanilla soy milk) with 1 slice whole-grain toast (4 grams) and 1 teaspoon jam
- Three-quarters cup raisin bran (6 grams) with 1 cup milk, 1 small banana (3 grams), and 2 tablespoons flaxseed (1.8 grams)
- Breakfast burrito with whole-wheat tortilla (5 grams), 1 ounce shredded cheese, ¼ cup nonfat refried beans or black beans (3.7 grams), ¼ avocado (3.4 grams), and 1 tablespoon salsa (.3 grams)

How Do I Get My Kid to Eat This Stuff?

If your child is used to snacking on chips and fruit snacks and eating his sandwiches on white bread, you might feel that switching him over to a high-fiber diet is impossible. It's not! It just may take some patience and diligence and maybe a little craftiness on your part. Here, Meredith Carter Conley and I offer some ideas.

- *Be a role model.* You can't expect your child to snack on sugar snap peas and hummus if you're munching on cheese puffs and a chocolate bar. Like kids, most adults are woefully short on fiber. In fact the average American woman gets only 12.1 to 13.8 grams of fiber per day, slightly less than the 14 grams recommended for the typical two-year-old. So consider this an opportunity to clean up your own eating habits.
- *Make changes gradually.* Start by offering foods that you know your child likes while adding a few new foods rather than subtracting her low-fiber favorites. Gradually reverse the ratio.
- *Go the stealth route.* Add veggie puree to spaghetti sauce your child likes. After he's enjoyed it a few times, let him know he's eaten the vegetables and lived to tell about it. Gradually make the puree chunkier, with even more veggies.
- *Keep trying.* Research shows that kids like what they know, so if you keep offering a child a certain food, eventually she will "know" it. It may take ten to fifteen exposures—it may take thirty!—before a child wants to eat red peppers or whole-grain pasta. Don't consider no a final answer.
- *Timing is everything.* Place a bowl of peas in front of your child when you know he's hungry or while he's waiting for his chicken nuggets to cook.
- *Serve foods with assembly required.* Have your child make her own fruit-and-yogurt parfaits: Set out small bowls of yogurt, fruit, and cereal with nuts, and have her spoon layers into a bowl. Or do a pizza night with whole-wheat dough or high-fiber English muffin halves, mozzarella, tomato sauce, and loads of veggies, like sliced peppers, shredded zucchini, or shredded carrots. Or, have your child create faces on whole-grain pancakes using peanut butter as glue and berries or banana slices for the eyes, nose, and mouth.
- *Find a superhero or athlete your child looks up to.* Then say, "Did you know Spider-Man gets his power from eating carrots?"

- *Offer choices, but not too many.* Ask: Do you want sweet potatoes or squash? Do you want to dip your apples in almond butter or peanut butter?
- *Don't label your child a "picky eater."* That can become a self-fulfilling prophecy. Your kid might actually enjoy black bean and corn salad or PB&J on whole-wheat bread, but you'll never know if you stick with ham and white bread.
- *Involve your child in planning meals and snacks.* Tell her, "You get to pick out the vegetable for tonight's dinner!"
- *Make sure your child eats breakfast.* It's hard to pack in those 14 plus fiber grams if you skip the morning meal.
- *Don't pressure.* The more you push high-fiber foods on a resistant child, the more he's likely to protest. Rewarding with treats—"If you eat two bites of broccoli, you can have ice cream"—isn't a wise approach, either, because it just makes the broccoli seem like a second-class citizen. Your kid might think, "Hmmm . . . this green stuff must be pretty bad if they're trying to bribe me with dessert."
- *Take your child food shopping.* The more involved she is in choosing the foods, the more invested she'll be in eating them. Offer choices. "Should we buy zucchini or squash? Red apples or green apples?" Make a fuss out of picking a new fruit or vegetable for the family to try. Play the color game: If your child loves purple, suggest that she find three purple fruits or vegetables, like grapes, eggplant, and purple onions.
- *Get your child involved in cooking.* Kids are more likely to eat foods they helped prepare. Even preschoolers can take part, though you'll have to be patient and have a broom and sponge at the ready. Have your child pour chopped veggies into a salad, help layer lasagna, drop blueberries into pancake batter, mash bananas for muffins, and help pack his lunch.

PACKAGED MUNCHIES WITH FIBER

Sure, carrots beat corn chips any day of the week, but if you look carefully, you can find high-fiber, nutritious choices among the thousands of crackers, chips, and other packaged snack foods on the market. Here are a few worthy choices:

Snack Food	Fiber Grams per Serving
Newman's Own Organics Thin Pretzel Sticks	4
Beanfields Bean and Rice Chips	4
Erin's All Natural Original Popcorn	3
Triscuits Hint of Salt Crackers	3
Food Should Taste Good All Natural Chips	3
Terra Sweets and Beet Chips	3

If you try these tips and still can't get your child's fiber intake up to necessary levels, consult a registered dietitian (RD) who specializes in working with kids. You can find an RD in your area through the American Dietetics Association website, eatright. org. You can get more terrific suggestions from Ellyn Satter's website ellynsatter.com and her book, *Secrets of Feeding a Healthy Family: How to Eat, How to Raise Good Eaters, How to Cook*. We also like Sally Kuzemchek's blog, realmomnutrition.com, and Amy Hendel's *The 4 Habits of Healthy Families: Everything Your Family Needs to Get Healthy and Stay Healthy for Life*.

———————

There's no question that boosting a child's fiber intake can go a long way toward minimizing constipation in a child who lives on chicken nuggets and mac and cheese. Still, one mistake I see many parents make is working very hard to improve their child's diet and then assuming the child's pooping habits are fine. Although eating a nutritious, fiber-rich diet is important for many obvious reasons, for a child with toileting issues it's typically not enough. Don't be afraid to add laxatives to an excellent diet if that's what your child needs. Having your child X-rayed for constipation will tell you whether your child needs to go that route.

CHAPTER 9

The Potty-Muscle Workout

If you've ever blown out a knee or wrenched a shoulder, you know how helpful physical therapy can be. But here's something most parents don't know: Physical therapy can help your kid pee and poop. At our clinic we have a team of physical therapists who specialize in helping kids retrain the muscles involved in using the toilet. Our therapists use many of the tools and techniques common in other types of physical therapy, including biofeedback, posture training, massage, stretching, and strengthening exercises. They have plenty of tricks up their sleeves, many of which you can help your child do at home. These techniques can make a huge difference for kids who have accidents, recurrent urinary tract infections (UTIs), constipation, or other potty problems related to holding poop or pee.

For this chapter I've collaborated with licensed physical therapists Ashley Silverman and Lori Baydush, who work with these kids every day. We've included a guide to perfect potty posture—yes, a few easy adjustments can help your kid stop straining and become a super pooper! We also explain how to give your child a colon massage and show four simple exercises that will help him relax on the toilet and fully empty both pee and poop.

We've found that children are quite receptive to these techniques, possibly more so than their parents. Sure, the idea of a potty workout seems strange at first, but the families we work with get comfortable quickly when they see the great results.

Finding the Potty Muscles

If you've done Kegels, you know which muscles we're talking about. Here's how we explain it to kids: These are the muscles you'd use if you were sitting in class and trying really hard not to fart (boys love that one) or if you were peeing and wanted to stop the flow. Technically, they're called the pelvic floor muscles, because they stretch across the bottom—a.k.a. "floor"—of the pelvis. But forget technicalities. Let's call them the "potty muscles."

Unlike, say, your biceps and glutes, the muscles involved in peeing and pooping aren't supposed to be powerhouses. You don't need them to lift a sofa or pedal a bike. They're mostly endurance muscles, assigned the unglamorous job of supporting your bladder, kidneys, intestines, and other internal organs. At rest these muscles remain minimally contracted, dutifully holding up your organs. When they are called to action for pooping or peeing, they relax to allow for full emptying.

At least they're supposed to. But many kids clench these muscles to hold in poop. Eventually all this holding inhibits their natural reflex to go—they no longer even feel the urge—and the stool piles up in the rectum. The upshot: The child ends up straining to push a big, hard poop through a small, tight hole. Ouch. Kids who hold pee also clench the potty muscles. They, too, lose touch with the emptying urge.

Many kids keep their potty muscles in a tightened state all day long, even when they're not on the toilet. Eventually the muscles fatigue, like an overstretched rubber band that has lost its elasticity, and poop just falls out or pee leaks out.

Here's what else can happen: Kids can lose coordination in these muscles or lose the ability to relax enough to fully empty their bladders or bowels. Ask these kids to relax their potty muscles and they may contract instead. We can watch the muscle mix-up firsthand when we hook up these kids to biofeedback machines that read muscle activity on a computer screen. The therapist places an electrode on either side of the child's bottom opening, and the child sits on a fake potty or lies on an exam table, attempting, on the therapist's instruction, to squeeze or relax. At our clinic kids can choose from several on-screen options: the squeezing and relaxing can make a rose close and open, make a dolphin jump out of the ocean and dive back in, or make a high-jumping athlete leap over a ball and then fall to the mat. Parents and kids alike are amazed to

---

POOPING TIP

Dogs flip their tails up to open and poop, right? Kids are similar: They need to keep their spines straight and tailbones pooched out, rather than tucked, so the pelvic muscles can open and let out poop.

watch the results: Very often, the child's muscles are working hard when they're not supposed to be working at all.

You don't necessarily need to bring your child to a physical therapist for biofeedback tests. If she's having ongoing pee or poop accidents, you can be pretty certain that her potty muscles need some rehab. Read on to learn strategies that will help.

Proper Pooping Posture

Plenty of modern inventions have improved life on Earth (praise the iPad!), but let me tell you: The toilet isn't one of them. Human beings were designed to squat. We've been doing it for all of human history—oh, about half a million years. Even today more than one billion people on the planet, mostly in Asia, the Middle East, and Africa, squat when they poop. I'd bet virtually none of them are constipated.

That's because your plumbing is not what it might seem. You might guess that sitting upright on the john would make gravity work in your favor, giving poop a straight shot downward. In fact, the reverse is true. When you stand, the rectum is bent (a position that helps keep poop safely inside); when you squat, the bend in the rectum straightens, and poop falls out easily, no pushing required. (Anyone who has been camping in the woods knows how easily you poop when you're forced to use the facilities in nature.) Sitting upright on the potty is a bit like trying to poop uphill.

Research proves that squatting beats sitting. In one telling study,[20] conducted by an Israeli doctor, subjects took two min-

20 Sikirov, D. Comparison of Straining During Defecation in Three Positions: Results

Figure 9-1 How your child should sit on the potty

utes and ten seconds to poop while sitting on a high toilet (no wonder we keep so much reading material on hand). But in a squat position they pooped in just fifty-one seconds and rated the experience as easier. Adding to the problem for children, toilets are too tall. With their feet dangling, kids may clench their inner thighs to keep from falling in. This clenching puts the pelvis in a position that tightens the bottom muscles, making relaxation even more difficult.

Your child would be better off, potty-wise, if he lived in Sri Lanka. But since your home probably has a toilet and not a hole in the ground, let's work with what we've got. One of the

and Implications for Human Health. *Digestive Diseases and Sciences.* Volume 48, Number 7, 1201-5.

best ways to help a kid who's constipated or holds pee is simply to change the way she sits on the potty, as shown in Figure 9-1.

Have her mimic a squatting posture by leaning forward and propping up her feet. Smaller kids may want to place a kid-size seat over the toilet so they don't feel like they're falling in.

Run down the following checklist when your child is on the toilet. (And try it yourself, while you're at it!) Your child should do the following:

- *Keep his hips and knees bent at ninety-degree angles.* His legs/knees should not slope downward. For most kids this requires elevating their feet on a stool.

- *Lean forward, elbows on knees, shoulders rounded but spine straight and tailbone pushed out rather than tucked.* This position places the rectum in a vertical position, giving your child the benefit of gravity, and stretches the abdominal cavity, giving the colon more room to pump stool to the rectum for emptying.

- *Keep his legs apart.* This helps the potty muscles fully relax.

Colon Massage

About fifteen minutes after you eat, when your stomach has stretched and digestion has begun, your colon revs up and you get the urge to poop. This urge is called the gastrocolic reflex. But in constipated kids the colon moves in slow motion, and often they don't feel the urge. You can help jumpstart this reflex by massaging your child's colon daily after a meal, ideally at the same time each day. Dinnertime tends to work best for families because of the after-breakfast rush to get off to school. See what works in your household. After school may also be a good time, because it's snack time and there is a big sense of relaxation after a stressful day.

Massaging the colon is a bit like squeezing a tube of toothpaste, section by section, in order to get the toothpaste to squirt out the end. One mom told me that fifteen minutes after she did a colon massage on her four-year-old son, "He pooped an elephant-size poop." Here's what to do:

- Have your child lay on his back on a bed or in a reclining chair.

- Using both hands, place your fingers on the child's lower right abdomen, just inside of the pelvic bone. (See Figure 9-2.) Gently press into his belly about one inch, and slowly sweep upward toward the ribcage for about two to three inches. Your child should be relaxed enough that you don't feel abdominal muscle resistance.

- Continue this pattern of pressing and sweeping in somewhat of a heart-shaped pattern: Go up along right side, across the bottom of the ribcage, then downward to just inside the left pelvic bone, and then progress back to center above the pubic bone. Tracing the entire colon should take about twenty seconds.

- Repeat the motion for five to ten minutes. Going slow and steady is key. Don't worry about how many revolutions you make.

- When you're done, have your child sit on the toilet for five to ten minutes.

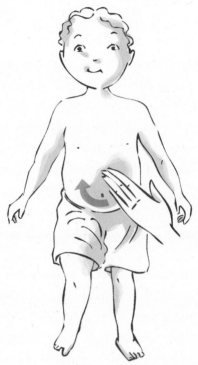

Figure 9-2
Massaging the colon

Potty Breathing

Remember *The Incredible Hulk* TV show, when Bill Bixby would grunt and groan, his neck veins bulging and throbbing, while he transformed into Lou Ferrigno? That's a bit like what a severely constipated kid does when he's trying to poop. All this straining causes the anal opening to tighten and close instead of relax and open.

To counteract this tightening of the potty muscles, instruct your child to blow out while pushing or to say "shhh" or "ggrrrrrrr." He can blow into his hands, but blowing into a toy works best for younger kids because it gives them a target. Your child can even blow a whistle or play the recorder!

Be sure your child blows slowly and gently, with puffy cheeks; this forces the potty muscles to relax and open more fully for complete emptying. Blowing hard, on the other hand, will cause these muscles to tighten. We tell kids to blow out of their mouth and their bottom at the same time. When they try this, they tell us, "Wow, that was so much better!"

Four Easy Exercises for Better Pooping and Peeing

Any kind of physical activity helps the colon move things along, so it's important to find activities your child enjoys that don't involve a TV or computer screen. (Sorry, Wii Golf doesn't count.) But sometimes exercise isn't enough. We see some incredibly fit kids who are star soccer players or tae kwon do black belts and yet are severely constipated; they've just gotten into the habit of holding their poop and their colons are operating in slow motion.

The four exercises shown here can help stretch tight potty muscles, improve posture to help with emptying, and strengthen muscles that have weakened or lost coordination due to holding. This "potty-muscle workout" is terrific for both poop and pee holders (and in reality most kids who hold pee are constipated as well) and can go a long way toward preventing accidents. Some of these exercises may remind you of yoga poses.

Aim to have your child perform these exercises daily, ideally at the same time of day so that the routine becomes a habit, like taking a bath or flossing. Supervise your child for several sessions to make sure she's doing the full program and executing the exercises correctly. Depending on her age, motivation, and maturity level, she may need supervision throughout the therapy period.

Frog Squat

This exercise mimics the squatting posture that's so helpful for using the toilet, stretching the pelvic muscles to prepare for pooping and peeing. Gravity helps relax the muscles, and the deep breathing prepares the child to go without straining. Aim to have your child do the frog squat before bed or at end of the day, when muscles are tightest. This will help him relax right before his last trip to the potty for the night.

- Instruct your child to squat down to the ground with feet wide apart, heels on the ground, knees spread wide, and hands on the ground like a sitting frog.

- Have your child look up, as if she is a frog looking for flies. Now, have her take deep breaths and be patient as she waits for the flies to come.

Figure 9-3 Frog Squat

- Tell your child to place her palms together with her elbows pushing against the insides of her knees or to keep her hands on the floor for balance. Have her straighten her back and lean slightly forward, feeling a gentle stretch between her legs.

- Have your child hold for ten to fifteen seconds. She can watch TV in this position or do the stretch five times, holding for fifteen counts each time.

Invisible Chair

This exercise strengthens the lower back muscles and helps train the child to keep his spine straight as he leans forward on the toilet. This exercise also stretches the potty muscles, which get tight from holding pee and poop and from all the time kids spend slumped over while playing video games.

- Have your child pretend that she is going to sit on a low chair, with feet shoulder-width apart, and have her reach her arms forward, tailbone pointing back. Instruct her to lower slowly until she is two or three inches above the chair, keeping her weight on her heels. Have her hover over the "chair" for five counts and then stand back up.

- Encourage your child do ten to fifteen repetitions twice a day.

Figure 9-4 Invisible Chair

Press-Up

This exercise strengthens the spinal muscles and stretches tight abdominals, reversing the slumped sitting posture so common among kids. The Press-Up also massages the colon and the tissue surrounding the bladder and rectum.

- Have your child lie on the floor on his belly with his palms flat on the floor under his shoulders. He should keep his hips and legs on the floor.

- Instruct your child to slowly press up his head, shoulders, and chest, as if peeling himself off the floor. Tell him to lift his head as high as he can, like a cobra getting ready to strike. Have him relax his belly when he is all the way up.

- Have him hold the position for five seconds and slowly lower to the starting position. Your child should do this stretch ten to fifteen times.

Figure 9-5 Press-Up on the belly

Figure 9-6 Kiddie Kegels

Kiddie Kegels

This exercise strengthens and improves the coordination of the potty muscles.

- Have your child sit with her legs crossed. Tell her to lean slightly forward so her back is straight and her elbows rest on her knees.

- Instruct your child to maintain this position for two or three seconds without holding her breath. In fact, to make sure she's not holding her breath, have her take a deep breath in, then exhale and count aloud as she squeezes her potty muscles. Tell her that as she pinches these muscles, she should imagine pulling the openings where her poop and pee come out up toward her belly button. Tell her not to squeeze her butt cheeks or tighten her abs or inner thighs. She should barely see any movement in her body if she's doing this exercise the right way.

- Have your child relax her potty muscles for five to ten seconds.

- Encourage your child to do this exercise ten times in a row several times a day.

Keeping a Potty Log

If you're like most parents of potty-trained kids, you're not standing outside the bathroom shouting, "Wait! Don't flush—let me come look!" I hate to break it to you, but that's actually what you should be doing. If your child has potty problems, no matter what his age, you need to be aware of what's going on in the bathroom.

Maintaining a potty log is a helpful way to keep tabs. Just as a workout diary keeps exercisers accountable and motivated, a potty log can provide insight into your child's toileting habits and help your family stick to the program. If you're not keeping track on paper (or on a computer), it's all too easy to skip the colon massage or the Invisible Chair exercise or forget how many times your child pooped yesterday or how often she peed.

A log will keep your family on track and provide a record of your child's progress. With tangible evidence of less straining, less pain, and fewer accidents, you and your child will gain confidence and feel even more motivated to stick with the plan.

Keeping a daily log also will increase communication between you and your child. It's important for parents to get in the habit of telling kids that peeing and pooping are natural and important. We call it "taking out the body's trash." An ongoing dialogue helps kids become less afraid to let it out when they need to. Some parents are, understandably, shy on this subject. It's a lot easier to say, "Hey, kiddo, how was your day at school?" than it is to say, "So, what did your poop look like?" Nevertheless, talking about this potty business helps kids become proud of their poop and pee rather than feel ashamed and hold it in. We're all for cheerleading when a child is successful on the toilet. You may even want to reward your child with stickers or other prizes for various potty accomplishments.

Make copies of the Potty Log on page 199. Some families find logging so helpful that they maintain a poop diary for six months. Others find that six weeks is long enough to see patterns and improvement. Charting is also a helpful tool for urologists; with a glance at your child's log, your doctor may be able to quickly identify the problems.

Following are tips for filling in the blanks. You can be as descriptive as you want in the log. Some parents make daily notes, such as "pooped at grandparents' house," "ate her vegetables well today," or "seems stressed about school." Make sure you keep track of the following:

- **Number of Poops:** Make a check mark each time your child poops. Remind your child to keep track of any pooping she does at school. Ideally, your child should poop once or twice a day, but at least four or five times a week.

- **Number on Bristol Stool Scale** (see Figure 2-1 on page 37): The scale, a depiction of the various healthy and unhealthy forms of poop, is explained in Chapter 2. We suggest taping a copy of the scale on the wall in your child's bathroom so he can easily refer to it. He'll quickly learn what shape poops correspond to which numbers. Have him jot a note at school so he doesn't forget what his poops looked like.

- **Strain to Empty:** Have your child answer yes or no.

- **Pain with Poop:** Again, yes or no.

- **Colon Massage:** Check when you perform the massage.

- **Number of Pees:** Your child should pee six to eight times each day. That's a lot to remember, so send your child to school with a small notebook or some other system for checking off each time she pees.

- **Daytime Accidents:** Indicate whether it was a poop or pee accident.

- **Nighttime Wetting:** Indicate yes or no.

A generation ago, doctors believed most toileting problems in children were caused by a congenital blockage in the urethra. In many cases, their solution was to operate, stretching a child's urethra with a metal rod and then sending him home, only to repeat the surgery a few months later because the problems remained. Now that we know better, urethra stretching seems a lot like bloodletting. It turns out that these kids simply were holding their poop and pee and were not relaxing their pelvic floor on the toilet. I still see an occasional mom who remembers having her bladder neck stretched as a child and asks me if I can perform the same operation on her daughter to cure her wetting problems.

Thankfully, science has progressed. We now treat holding with laxatives and emptying at regular intervals, and we treat tight pelvic floor muscles with physical therapy techniques, including those described in this chapter. Learning to relax these muscles is an important component of therapy for wetting problems. This stuff works!

POTTY LOG

	Sunday	Monday	Tuesday	Wednesday	Thursday	Friday	Saturday
Number of Poops							
Number on Bristol Stool Scale							
Strain to Empty							
Pain with Poop							
Colon Massage							
Number of Pees							
Daytime Accidents (pee or poop)							
Nighttime Wetting							

Notes:

CHAPTER 10

Six Strategies to Help Your Child Stick with the Program

Explaining to parents why their child is having toileting troubles is one of the best parts of my job. Not that folks love to hear, "Your son has a tennis ball–size mass of poop in his rectum," but when Mom and Dad learn that their child's problems are caused by constipation or holding pee, rather than a nerve disorder or sheer defiance, they're relieved. Sometimes they're thrilled. Sometimes they even hug me. Typically they are eager to start the therapies I prescribe and put the accidents, bedwetting, or infections behind them.

Ah, but sometimes the child has her own agenda, putting a glitch in the plan. Though older children tend to be more cooperative with the treatment, preschool-age children often resist. They may not even realize or particularly care that they have a problem, and, of course, they don't appreciate the long-term consequences of leaving a hyperactive bladder untreated. Plus, toileting troubles tend to surface just when kids are in the throes of asserting their independence. I've had parents report all kinds of resistance. One of my patients poured her laxative-laced apple juice on the kitchen floor—and gave her mom that "What are you gonna do about it?" grin. Another patient pretends not to notice when her potty watch vibrates. Every day I hear from parents, "When I tell my kid it's time to sit on the toilet, she screams, 'Noooo!!! I *don't* have to go!' and stomps off."

I have two preschoolers of my own—I live this kind of stuff every day. And like many dads, I'm a pushover. Sometimes I cave in when my daughters won't pick up their dirty clothes or put on their shoes and I just do the job myself. But when your child has bladder or bowel problems, caving isn't an option (plus, it won't exactly help to drink your child's laxative). The fact is, the longer a child's colon remains stretched or his bladder remains hyperactive, the more difficult these troubles are to resolve. Getting your child on board with the program is important.

Parents are always asking me, "So what am I supposed to *do?*" I'm often at a loss to answer, especially since I know that high-pressure tactics usually backfire. In many cases pressure to potty train too early is what caused, or exacerbated, the very problems we're trying to solve. Still, there are ways to win a child's cooperation without putting undue stress on her. To explain these strategies, I have collaborated with Linda Nicolotti, Ph.D., a Winston-Salem child psychologist who counsels children with toileting problems. In this chapter we suggest several techniques for helping your child comply with her treatment plan. When you choose from among them, take into account your child's age, developmental level, personality, and family situation. You'll probably need a combination of approaches. Know that what works at one stage of the treatment might lose its effectiveness the next, so be flexible and modify your strategies as needed. Some kids get on board right away, whereas others meet new strategies with, "No!" So be consistent and give each strategy a real chance.

Rest assured, things will get better. In my experience if you can coax children into complying just enough for them to notice progress, like having fewer accidents, they become increasingly willing to follow through. But then again some children misconstrue progress as a sign that their problems are solved and that they no longer need to take laxatives or sit on the potty every two hours. Kids are complicated!

Strategy #1:
Give Your Child Information—But Not Too Much

I don't recommend telling a four-year-old, "If you don't void every two hours, your bladder capacity will remain compromised, and you may develop pelvic pain in college." Too much information will only confuse a child and bore the heck out of her; it definitely won't motivate her to sit on the toilet. On the other hand, some children are quite interested in, and capable of, understanding what's happening inside

WHEN TO SEE A THERAPIST

If, after a good-faith effort lasting several weeks, you haven't hit on a technique that gets your child peeing and pooping regularly, taking his laxatives, or following any other aspect of treatment, seek help from a child psychologist or other mental health specialist.

Find help sooner if you feel overwhelmed and want immediate support, if your child's potty issues are already serious and impacting her health, or if you are deadlocked in a power struggle with your child or are in conflict with your spouse over your child's potty problems. I find that parents often blame each other when a child develops toileting problems— or, worse, they blame the child. A therapist can help you move past blame and onto practical solutions.

I also recommend seeing a therapist from the get-go if your child has complicating mental-health or emotional problems, such as Attention-Deficit/Hyperactivity Disorder (ADHD), Oppositional Defiant Disorder (ODD), or anxiety or mood disorders. A therapist experienced with toileting troubles can offer suggestions more suited to your family's situation.

Counseling needn't be a long-term, expensive proposition. A few sessions may be all it takes to get your family on track. An experienced mental health provider can thoroughly assess your family's issues and help your child better manage stress, anxiety, or anger that may be stemming from her potty problems. A therapist also can provide emotional support to your family.

Good sources for appropriate referrals include your pediatrician, school counselor, state psychological association, or health insurance company.

their bodies. When children ask questions like, "How does the pee get into my body?" it usually means they can handle more information. On the other hand, when they change the topic or look away, that's your sign to back off. You may need to repeat the information at a later time to make sure the important stuff sticks.

Demonstrations can help kids understand what's happening in their bodies. For example, if your child is constipated, try cutting the toe off a sock to create a tube and fill the tube with rolled-up socks. Explain the process something like this: "This tube is like your intestine and the sock balls are like poop. Every time you eat, more socks go into the tube; if you don't keep pooping them out, eventually the tube runs out of room and has to stretch. This stretching can give you a tummy ache and makes the socks get stuck. Sometimes, so many socks get piled up that some are pushed out. That's like having a poop accident."

In our clinic one of the most helpful analogies is comparing poop to trash. I'll say, "You know how you have to take the trash out regularly or it all piles up? Well, it's the same deal with poop." That seems to hit home. Almost universally kids don't like the idea of garbage accumulating in their bodies.

If your child is having wetting accidents, fill a balloon until it overflows and explain that water spilling out is like having an accident. If your child's accidents are due to constipation, as most are, try this experiment: Place two identical glasses on a tray with a lip and pour water into the glasses until they are three-quarters full. Let your child measure the water; she'll have fun with it. Explain that the water represents pee in the bladder. Now, have your child start dropping marbles or small rocks into one of the glasses. The marbles represent poop in the intestines. Watch as the water overflows when too many marbles are dropped into the glass and explain that this is also how her body works. Too much poop in the intestines squishes the bladder, causing pee to spill out. She can avoid this overflow by pooping regularly.

Look for a basic physiology book that's appropriate for your child's age. *Everyone Poops* is a favorite for many families, but if it's too basic for your child, check your library for children's books that explain how drinking and eating lead to peeing and pooping.

Strategy #2:
Have Your Doctor Talk Directly to Your Child

As most parents have experienced, children often listen best to anyone besides Mom or Dad. Doctors tend to rate highly in kids' eyes, so make an appointment with your pediatrician to devise a treatment plan based on this book, and have the doctor explain the plan to your child in kid-friendly terms while looking him in the eye. In my experience some doctors direct the entire conversation to the parents, ignoring the five-year-old drawing with crayons in the corner—the patient. Be sure your child is engaged during the explanation.

Then, when you're home, you can say, "Remember, Dr. Mills says you need to take your MiraLAX so that your poop won't get stuck in your body," or "Dr. Chun says you have to try to poop after dinner."

Strategy #3:
Offer Positive Reinforcement

Call it a reward, a prize, an inducement, or a bribe—for most kids, it works, much better than threatening and definitely better than yelling. Rewards help children stay motivated when they are doing something difficult for them. After all, isn't this the whole point—getting your child to learn new skills so she can be healthier?

For a reward to be effective, it has to be something your child really, really covets. Think of it this way: *Does Isaac want the MatchBox car enough to sit on the potty after meals?* To make sure you're offering a reward that's meaningful to your child, let him help choose it. Rewards need not break the bank. Let him pick out a couple of books or a DVD at the library and offer an extra bedtime story or video viewing as a prize. Take your child to the resale store and let her pick out a toy. (It's amazing how excited a four-year-old can get over a thirty-five-cent racecar.) The prospect of playing a board game with you or reading for ten extra minutes can be very enticing. Just make sure your child doesn't get the same or similar rewards without accomplishing his goal. Change up the rewards as needed so they don't lose their sparkle.

Rewards work best if you give them immediately after they're earned, especially with the toddler and preschool-aged crowd. A child with a short attention span may lose interest if he has to wait all day to receive his prize. You might try a two-tiered reward system, with both immediate and longer-term rewards. For example, every time your child sits on the potty, he gets to place a sticker on his chart. When he earns seven stickers, he gets the grand prize, like the extra bedtime story. Keep the chart simple and be consistent.

Start with a goal you know your child can accomplish easily so she can experience immediate success and gratification. Once your child consistently accomplishes the initial goal, gradually set the bar higher. For instance start by rewarding her simply for sitting on the potty, then later for actually peeing or pooping.

In addition to rewarding your child, offer verbal praise that is specific to the goal your child is working on. Look your child in the eye, and along with the praise, offer a loving touch and a warm smile. As with rewards, offer praise right away. For example, "I like that you paid attention to your watch and went to the bathroom on your own." Be genuine and express enthusiasm without going over the top. A generic "good job" will go in one ear and out the other. Plus your child may have no idea what he did a good job for. It may help to report your child's progress to a family member. Say, "Let's call Daddy and tell him you did all of your potty exercises!" Eventually, the actions you're rewarding and praising your child for will become second nature, and you can phase out the rewards.

Strategy #4:
Remain Calm—And Help Your Child Do the Same

If you feel like yelling, "Get your butt on the *#$%&*ing potty!!" you'd hardly be the first parent to experience that feeling. You wouldn't be the first to act on it, either, but try hard not to. Raising your voice will only make your child less interested in complying. Besides, that's not the kind of behavior you want your child to model, right? Since you're more likely to lose your temper if you're tired or stressed out, do what you can to take care of yourself, whether that's taking a yoga class, having a pizza date night with your spouse, escaping for an hour with a book or guilty-pleasure TV show, or going to bed earlier so you can get more sleep.

What can you do when your child absolutely refuses to sit on the toilet, even though she's just had three accidents and you're about to blow a gasket? Stop in your tracks and take slow deep breaths, expanding your abdomen as you inhale. Do some muscle relaxation, too, starting with your head and working your way down your body, noticing which muscles are tense, and relaxing each muscle one by one. Practicing these relaxation strategies when you're not upset will help you calm down faster during a heated moment. In addition to preempting a blowout, this is great stuff to demonstrate for your child. If you feel that you're about to lose your cool and are unable to stop yourself with deep breathing, step away for a few moments, explaining to your child that you'll be right back. If you do blow up in front of your child, apologize. Try, "Gosh, I'm sorry I lost my temper. I shouldn't have done that. Let's handle it a different way." Go easy on yourself. What seems obvious and utterly rational to a parent may make no sense to a five-year-old, and that can be hard for parents to cope with.

At the same time, have empathy for your child, and help him work through his feelings. He may be lashing out because his body isn't cooperating, because he's embarrassed about the accidents, or because he's tired of having to do things, like take laxatives or use a bedwetting alarm, that his siblings and friends don't have to do.

Encourage your child to express feelings through words. She may need help identifying her feelings and expressing them verbally. Let's say your child yells, "No, I don't want to!" when you remind her, while she's working on an art project, that it is time to sit on the potty. If she needs help finding the words to express her feelings, say, "It looks like you are feeling angry because you don't want to use the toilet right now. Can you tell me more about how you are feeling?" If she has trouble pinpointing her feelings, you can show her emotion flash cards (cards that indicate emotions with pictures and words) and say, "Find a card that shows how you are feeling right now." Or try a game of emotion charades. Practice this when your child isn't angry. Take turns acting out different emotions, such as anger or impatience, with corresponding facial expressions and behaviors.

Give your child a "tool kit" to cope with negative emotions, like that deep breathing and muscle relaxation you earlier demonstrated (right?). Other tools include quiet activities such as drawing, coloring, reading, and listening to music, or physical activities such as jogging in place or jumping jacks. Have your child help come up with a list of strategies, and post the list in his room as a reminder. Gather all of the materials your child will need in his tool kit for easy access when those emotions flare. When you notice your child becoming upset, cue him to use the strategies in his tool kit.

Strategy #5:
Introduce Potty Play
Play isn't just fun for kids. It also can be a way for them to master new skills, express emotions, and resolve conflicts—all of which makes play a terrific way for kids to overcome toileting challenges. Helpful toys include a doll with a toy potty, a furnished dollhouse (make sure it has a bathroom!) with a doll family that lives in the house, action figures, puppets, and stuffed animals. You can even find dolls that pee and poop! Girls and boys alike enjoy these types of toys.

To help your child reinforce potty skills and practice expressing emotions, hand her a favorite doll, stuffed animal, or action figure, and say, "How does your doll feel about going poop on the potty? Oh, and I wonder why is that? What do you think would make it easier for your doll to poop on the potty? I wonder if your doll would have an easier time going poop on the potty if she [fill in physician recommendations]. Let's teach her!"

Some children are more receptive to learning and practicing a new skill if the instruction is not targeted directly at them. A doll and potty are handy in this situation. Try teaching the doll the skill and then have your child repeat the lesson with the doll. Say, "Let's set the timer and teach your doll to sit on the potty when the timer goes off."

Finally, to make your child happier and more relaxed on the toilet, let her read a favorite book, hold a doll she adores, or play a video game. These activities might also serve as positive reinforcement for following through with her treatment plan.

Strategy #6:
Offer Plenty of Choices and Foster Autonomy

When a child wets his bed or has chronic toileting accidents, he's likely to feel frustrated by the lack of control over his body. Giving him more autonomy, both in toileting decisions and in other areas in life, can help compensate.

For example, instead of reminding your child to use the toilet every two hours, have her wear a potty watch (see Chapter 3). Offer options such as: "Do you want to set your watch for the hour or the half-hour?" "Do you want to use the bathroom upstairs or downstairs?" "Do you want to bring your stuffed alligator or tiger into the bathroom?"

At the same time, make an effort to give your child autonomy in other aspects of her life, so she feels a sense of control and doesn't feel like her entire existence revolves around the potty. If she picks out clothes that don't match, fine, who cares? Let her bathe herself, even if she doesn't get all the dirt scrubbed off her toes. Let her help choose the dinner menu and help layer the lasagna.

EXTRA HELP FOR KIDS WITH ATTENTION-DEFICIT/ HYPERACTIVITY DISORDER

Think about what it takes to pee and poop appropriately: You need to recognize your body's urges, stop whatever you're doing and walk to another room, remember why you're there, and do something tedious for as long as it takes to finish the job. That's a tall order for most young children, but it's particularly challenging for children with Attention-Deficit/Hyperactivity Disorder (ADHD), who have trouble focusing on boring tasks and keeping information in mind long enough to complete the job. So it's no surprise that these kids have higher rates of toileting troubles and more difficulty complying with the treatments.

A child with ADHD may have difficulty listening to his body's signals that it's time to go, especially when other, more fun things are happening. En route to the bathroom, he may become distracted by the train set in the corner and never make it to the toilet. What's more, children with ADHD tend to live in the moment and often fail to see future events approaching, much less plan for them. Of course, when you have a full bladder or bowel, some foresight and planning are necessary to avoid accidents. ADHD also involves difficulties with self-motivation, so it can be tough for a child with this disorder to take responsibility for following his treatment plan.

Here are tips for getting your child with ADHD to stick with the program.

- *Make sure your child's ADHD is adequately diagnosed and treated.* Treatment might involve a behavior-management program, parenting strategies, self-control training, and medication. In addition to the ADHD and toileting problems, your child may also be dealing with academic problems, social challenges, oppositional behavior, and anxiety or mood problems, which also require the appropriate assessment and treatment. Your pediatrician and a qualified mental health professional can help guide you through the maze of diagnoses and treatment strategies for ADHD and associated issues.
- *Use rewards, accompanied by praise.* A positive approach is important to bolster the behavior you're looking for. We explain how to implement rewards and

praise elsewhere in this chapter. If you find it necessary to give negative consequences, make them mild. ("I am going to count to three. If you don't start walking to the potty by the time I get to three, then your truck will be in time-out for five minutes.") Be sure to reward your child at least three times as often as you give consequences. Give praise, rewards, and consequences swiftly and consistently. Make sure both you and any other caregivers respond in the same way.

- *Maximize structure.* Have a potty schedule posted where your child will see it, like the toy cabinet, and give verbal reminders in addition to having your child wear a potty alarm watch. If your child has difficulty with transitions, set your own alarm as well and give her five minutes' notice before it's time for her to use the toilet again. Use a chart listing daily goals, rewards for completing goals, and consequences for not completing goals.

- *Make using the potty more interesting.* Give your son a target to aim for in the toilet, like Cheerios or a piece of toilet paper. Have toys or books for him to play with or look at while he's on the toilet.

- *Give short, direct commands.* Don't spend time reasoning with your child. Make sure you have her attention and minimize distractions. When it's time for her to use the potty, get down on her level and look her in the eye. Make sure she sets her toys aside or turns off the TV, and say, "Your potty alarm went off. It is time for you to go sit on the toilet."

- *Help your child recognize the urge to poop or pee.* Try, "It might feel like pressure in your bottom," or "When you start squatting down or crossing your legs, that means you have to go to the bathroom." Then, when you see your child doing this, you can say, "I see you're squatting down. What did we say that means?" If your child is squatting and claims he doesn't need to go, say, "Well, let's go to the bathroom and try, anyway. Remember, you'll get a sticker on your chart, and you'll be closer to getting that toy!"

- *Make the toileting program part of your child's 504 plan.* Have your child's teacher remind her about her toileting goals, record her progress on the chart, and praise her for her progress. Have the school chart come home daily with your child, and transfer the results to your home chart. Supply your child's teacher with all the necessary supplies, and meet with the teacher outside of class to explain it all. A gift card for the teacher's extra time and effort might go a long way as well.

If those kinds of choices don't work, you may have to offer tougher choices in the form of a consequence, such as: "You can either choose to sit on the potty by the time I count to three and earn a sticker on your chart, or if you choose not to sit on the potty, I will have to take away your fire truck. Which choice do you want to make?" I know that sounds harsh, and no parent wants to pressure a child into using the toilet, but consequences may be what it takes to persuade a strong-willed child to sit on the potty. Be sure to use a calm voice, follow through, and be consistent with the rules; otherwise what you say will have no power. Consequences also show your child that you are dead serious about his treatment. He will likely feel some comfort in knowing that you consistently enforce the doctor's rules. Children need to test limits and know that the boundaries are still in place. Tell your child, "I'm doing this because I care about you, and I want your body to be healthy, and this is what Dr. Smith says your body needs to stay healthy."

You probably can think of a thousand things that are more fun to do than persuading your child to sit on the potty when she's not interested or certain that she doesn't need to go. And you may not be thrilled by the prospect of being more insistent than you feel is warranted or in your nature. I understand! Your child may not ever comply happily with these therapies, but the important thing is that he complies. You are protecting your child's health.

Acknowledgments

We are indebted to the Rosso family for allowing us to include Zoe's case in this book and to Dr. Sean O'Regan for taking the time to speak to us about his remarkable research. We also are grateful to Bailey Hooten, Dee Carter, and Cici Carter for sharing their stories.

Linda Nicolotti, Ph.D., Ashley Silverman, P.T., and Lori Baydush, P.T., went above and beyond, generously sharing their wisdom and expertise in psychology and physical therapy, respectively, as well as their valuable time. Meredith Carter Conley, R.D., provided a wealth of knowledge for the nutrition chapter, and Tom Keating, Ph.D., blew us away with his passion for and knowledge of school bathroom issues.

Many thanks to Stacy Whitman and Sarah Bowen Shea for their astute suggestions and to Dr. John Fortunato and physical therapist Terry Sink for their helpful advice.

To our editor, Lara Asher: Thanks a million for believing in our idea. Of course, we also appreciate the hard work and persistence of our agent, Jane Dystel.

Index

A

accidents, daytime, 65–89
  advice for parents, 76–80, 82
  bladder-relaxing medication, 83–84, 86
  and constipation, 3, 70–72
  and holding pattern, xii–xiii, 69, 72–77
  measuring bladder capacity, 81, 94–97
  pain and toileting, 89
  psychological components of, 88
  vaginal voiding, 86–87
activity. *See* physical activity
alpha1-blockers, 84, 86
Anthony, Evelyn, 40, 93
attention deficit/hyperactivity disorder (ADHD), 88, 203, 212–13
  and bed-wetting, 92, 103, 105
Aveeno, 117, 121

B

baths, 117, 129

Baydush, Lori, 182
bed-wetting, xiii, 66, 90–107
  and ADHD, 92, 103, 105
  bed-wetting alarms, 102–4
  bladder capacity/hyperactivity, 94–97, 99–100
  and constipation, 3, 93, 96, 97–98
  genetic marker of, 91, 92
  medical causes of, 93–94
  producing excess urine, 104–7
  and UTIs, 93–94
  what not to do, 100, 101
Benefiber, 60
bladder. *See also* urinary problems, 73–74
  affect of constipation, 12, 15, 43–46, 70, 96, 97–98
  affect of holding, 69, 73–76
  and brain, 68–69
  capacity and hyperactivity of, 87, 94–97, 99–100
  medication for relaxing, 83–84, 86
  and UTIs, 109–10

W

wetting. *See* accidents, daytime; bed-wetting

White, Ryan, 132

X

X-rays, for children, 31–33

Y

Yazbeck, Salam, 9, 10

About the Authors

Steve J. Hodges, M.D., is a fellowship-trained pediatric urologist and associate professor of pediatric urology at Wake Forest University School of Medicine in Winston-Salem, North Carolina. He sees three thousand children per year at the university's Department of Urology. Dr. Hodges has authored numerous textbook chapters and articles in peer-reviewed journals. Dr. Hodges was the first to organize comprehensive care for children with dysfunctional elimination at Wake Forest Baptist Health, bringing together the disciplines of urology, gastroenterology, psychology, and physical therapy. Dr. Hodges is married to registered dietitian Jennifer Hodges, R.D., L.D.N., and they have three young girls. In addition to Dr. Hodges's clinical encounters with frustrated families, his own experiences with constipation as a child and the process of toilet training his own children have made the study of dysfunctional elimination a personal passion for him.

Suzanne Schlosberg is known for her frank and funny take on health and parenting topics. She is the author or coauthor of a dozen books, including *Fitness for Dummies*, *The Ultimate Workout Log*, *The Ultimate Diet Log*, and *The Good Neighbor Cookbook*. Her articles have appeared in *Parents*, *Parenting*, *Fit Pregnancy*, *American Baby*, *Ladies' Home Journal*, and numerous other media outlets. Schlosberg lives in Bend, Oregon, with her husband and four-year-old twin boys. Her website is www.suzanneschlosberg.com.